ANTON CHEKHOV

WORLD DRAMATISTS

ANTON
HEKHOV

PG
3458
.m3713

SIEGFRIED MELCHINGER

Translated by Edith Tarcov

WITH HALFTONE ILLUSTRATIONS

FREDERICK UNGAR PUBLISHING CO.
NEW YORK

Translated from the German Anton Tschechow
*Published by arrangement with Friedrich Verlag,
Velber, Germany*

*Copyright © 1972 by Frederick Ungar Publishing Co., Inc.
Printed in the United States of America
Library of Congress Catalog Number: 76-163146
Designed by Edith Fowler
ISBN: 0-8044-2615-5 (cloth)*

lh 6-28

CONTENTS

CHRONOLOGY

1860   January 29, Chekhov is born in Taganrog, on the Sea of Asov.

1876   Chekhov's father goes bankrupt. Family moves to Moscow. Chekhov remains in Taganrog by himself to finish his high-school education there.

1879   Chekhov begins to study medicine in Moscow.

1881   Chekhov publishes first work, in newspapers.

1881–84   Chekhov works on "Play without a Title" (*Platonov*).

1884   Chekhov receives his M.D. *Melpomene*, his first collection of stories, is published.

1885   *Motley Tales*, second volume of collected stories, is published.

1887   *Ivanov* produced at the Korsh Theater. One-acter *Swan Song* (also called *Kalkhas*) produced.

1888   *Ivanov* is performed in Saint Petersburg. Chekhov is awarded the Pushkin Prize by the Imperial Academy. One-acter *The Bear* is produced.

1889   One-acter *The Proposal* is produced. No-
        vella *The Steppe* is published. Third volume
        of collected stories is published. *The Wood
        Demon* is performed at a private theater in
        Moscow.

1890   One-acters *The Wedding* and *A Tragedian
        in Spite of Himself* produced. Chekhov goes
        to Sakhalin. *Through Siberia* is published.

1891   One-acter *The Jubilee* (also called *The Anni-
        versary*) is produced. Chekhov travels
        through Europe.

1892   Chekhov is appointed district physician in a
        province in which famine and cholera are
        raging. He acquires an estate in Melikhovo.

1894   Publication of the report *Sakhalin*.

1896   *The Sea Gull* is performed in Saint Peters-
        burg.

1897   Chekhov's tuberculosis becomes acute. *Uncle
        Vanya* is on tour in Russia's provinces.
        Chekhov spends winter in the south of
        France.

1898   *The Sea Gull* is performed in Moscow.
        Chekhov takes a house in the Crimea.

1899   *Uncle Vanya* is performed in Moscow.
        Chekhov moves to Yalta.

1900   Chekhov becomes a member of the Imperial
        Academy.

1901   *The Three Sisters* is performed in Moscow.
        Chekhov marries Olga Knipper.

1902   Chekhov resigns from the Imperial Academy
        because Gorky's nomination was vetoed
        upon the order of Nicholas II.

1904   *The Cherry Orchard* is performed in Mos-
        cow.
        July 15, in Badenweiler, Germany, Chekhov
        dies.

A NECESSARY FOREWORD

Chekhov's material was life. Though he drew heavily on his observations of others, he did use his own life as source material, but only when it seemed to him "interesting" to others. He never wrote a line for the sake of writing, and never wrote a line about anything he did not understand. "Only imbeciles and charlatans," he said, "believe that they understand everything."

Chekhov's objective was to extract from his material, which he mastered and shaped, its inherent truth: life. "Above all, my friends," he said, "one must never lie. . . . In art, one cannot lie. . . . In love, in politics, in medicine, one can deceive men and even the dear Lord. . . . In art, that is impossible." When critics berated him for the lack of a plan or program, saying that his stories lacked the element of social protest, that his plays betrayed his "indifference," he was indignant.

"Don't I protest," he answered, "from the beginning to the end, from the first line to the last, against the lie?" His most sacred tenet was "abso-

3

lute freedom, freedom from force and from lies, however they may be expressed." Truth, as he understood it, is synonymous with justice. "Of all the men I have known," Gorky wrote to him, "you, I believe, are the first who is truly free and bows before nothing."

If Chekhov could now read what is written about him in so many books—that he was the great observer of his epoch, an epoch in decline, the turn of the century—he would burst into sarcastic laughter. His contemporaries feared his sharp tongue. The innumerable letters he wrote are full of vitriolic and pertinent comments. (In the twenty-volume Russian edition of Chekhov's collected works, the letters take up volumes 13–20.) Each of them proves that he was not merely observing what was before him but also looking through and behind it.

Chekhov did not merely describe. Although his material was always life itself, he was well aware of the difference between a representation of life and mere description, or faithful reproduction, of life. If one examines carefully his observations about the various productions of his plays, it becomes clear that he did not live to see a single play produced on the stage as he visualized it while writing it. He expressed dissatisfaction with the Moscow Art Theater production of *The Sea Gull*, because the director—none other than Stanislavsky himself—had decked it out with a mass of realistic detail. "Realistic?" Chekhov exclaimed. "But the theater is art!" And, as if to slap the ideologues of the theater of his day, he added, "You forget, you don't have a fourth wall!"

Chekhov's method has been compared to that of Cézanne, and rightly so. His plan was not that of presenting truth itself, but rather of presenting a representation of truth. He once spoke of the "quintessence," which it was his aim to show. "One must discard everything that is superfluous," he said. But he lived in a loquacious epoch, and his contemporaries took his laconism for harshness. And so Chekhov, who struggled and searched for this laconism, this quality of terseness and brevity, had to witness productions of his plays that were stuffed with the "superfluous." Later, Stanislavsky recognized that the Chekhov presented by the Moscow Art Theater had not been the true or the whole Chekhov. Stanislavsky himself reported a telling comment the playwright made to him: "You know," Chekhov said, "I shall write a new play that will begin with these lines: 'How wonderfully quiet it is here. Not a bird is heard. Not a dog barks. Not a cuckoo cries, not an owl hoots, not a nightingale is singing. Not a clock is striking, and not a single cricket chirping!' "

Chekhov's laconic presentation aims to bring out the quintessence of the play. Therefore, the material must not in any way be manipulated—not for the sake of a lesson or moral, not for an ideology, philosophy, or religion.

Shortly before his death, Chekhov wrote to his wife, "You ask me, 'What is life?' That is just as if you asked, 'What is a carrot?' A carrot is a carrot, and one knows no more about it." He admired Zola and loved Tolstoy, yet he reproached both for judging and writing about matters they did not understand.

Biographers who try to deduce Chekhov's views from his characters' observations should keep in mind what he wrote in one of his letters: "When a cup of coffee is set before you, you don't try to find beer in it. When I set before you the thoughts of the Professor [in *Uncle Vanya*], listen well, and don't search in them for the thoughts of Chekhov."

Even his letters are full of contradictory observations. They were not written for publication; they are expressions of his temperament, of his states of mind and his physical health, of his fleeting thoughts. Above all, they are words addressed to particular persons. Chekhov had an uncommon sensitivity to people. Speaking of one of his characters, he said that there are various talents, talents for writing, for acting, for painting, but that this person was endowed with a special talent—"A talent for human beings. . . . he could reflect in his soul upon the suffering of others." Nothing could be more misleading than to make deductions about Chekhov himself from this description of one of his characters. It would never have occurred to Chekhov to say this of himself. First of all, unlike this character, he had a talent for writing. It is also true, as people who knew him admit, that in conversation, when in earnest about his subject, he could be harsh and even wounding. Yet, the quotation proves that Chekhov knew well this "talent for human beings." It was one of the human potentials he found in others and in himself—and so he used it as material.

From passages in his letters the conclusion was drawn that, despite his previous statements and observations, Chekhov, toward the end of his life, became religious. But these passages are from letters addressed to religious persons whose feelings he respected. Yet his tact was not always without irony. Once he said, "Of course we shall live on after death; immortality is a fact. Just wait," he added, and one can see him smile, "I shall prove it to you one day quite clearly."

He believed only what could be proved. "It is not hard to believe in God," begins a passage the censor struck from a story. "The Inquisitors, too, believed in Him. Biron [the feared minister of the Czarina

Anna Ivanovna] and Arkatshev [who organized the reaction under Alexander I] also believed. No, let us believe in man!" But this view, too, became material for his writing.

Dr. Chekhov did not put much faith in mankind. "For each intelligent human being, there are a thousand numskulls. And the majority of the intelligentsia is hypocritical, false, hysterical, and lazy." He mistrusted philosophies—"The devil take the philosophy of the great ones of this world!" Yet he did not deny that progress had improved and would further improve the living conditions of the people. "Reflection and justice tell me," he said, writing against Tolstoy, "that there is more love of our fellowmen in the inventions of electricity and steam than in chastity and in abstinence from the enjoyment of eating meat."

For a time, Soviet academicians tried to prove that Chekhov was a forerunner of the 1917 Revolution, and found proof for it in his characters' observations. Ilya Ehrenburg, in the remarkable essay "On Re-reading Chekhov" (1961), put this matter to rights: "Chekhov never held precisely defined political ideas, and I have no intention of ascribing to him a Marxist world view. Yet we have the right to consider him the first artist who was of the twentieth century." Ehrenburg emphasized Chekhov's "topicality," and said it was based on his "active work against misery, against injustice and lies."

And here I come to the most important point: I know of no other writer who lived so rigorously by the maxims of his art. Chekhov acted as a matter of course, without talking about it. In "Anton Chekhov: An Essay," Thomas Mann praised his modesty and called it his most outstanding characteristic; but I do not see Chekhov as modest. He knew exactly who he was and what others were. He did not hesitate to criticize Tolstoy, and to say of Zola that he did not think of him as a great writer. He was repelled by Dostoyevsky, and he recognized the weaknesses in the writings of Gorky, whom he loved as a human being and defended politically. "Gorky," he said, "has no idea of architecture. He doesn't know how to build." ("Each sentence has to be built and constructed," he wrote to a woman writer. "In this lies the whole art.")

What gives the impression of modesty is really a complete lack of posturing. He was far too busy, working indefatigably in his constant commitment to aid the poor and the suffering. And all his work was done as a matter of course. We know now that in his twenty-third year he began to suffer from attacks of the tuberculosis he eventually was to die of. Yet, though he was well aware that he was tubercular, he hurried into the districts ravaged by starvation and cholera, to do, as he said, his work as a physician. In the last year of his life, 1904, when the Russo-Japanese war broke out, his first thought was to volunteer for service as an army doctor at the front. And when, having risen from the abject poverty of his childhood and youth to a level of comfortable affluence, he acquired a country estate, he treated patients from the surrounding villages without charge. Soon, of course, he was being visited by a great many of them.

Knowing that ignorance was one of the causes of Russia's misery, he financed three schools. He set up hospitals for indigent tuberculosis patients.

And he undertook a one-man expedition to a place harder to penetrate than the jungle: he went to Sakhalin, a cold, bleak island between the Tatar Strait and the Sea of Okhotsk, which was used for penal colonies by the Russian government. After a three-month journey through Siberia and a three-month stay on the island, he published a report of the conditions under which the deportees on Sakhalin lived. As a result, some of the worst abuses were remedied. His experiences on Sakhalin is a central subject in his autobiographical writings. The memories of this "hell" haunted Chekhov for years— Chekhov who, in his own words, "could write only what was based on memories." At the time, Strindberg was undergoing his very personal inferno, and Tolstoy was proclaiming his message of love for one's fellowmen. Out of their experiences both Strindberg and Tolstoy created literature. Chekhov, however, felt that one did not write fiction about Sakhalin; instead, he wrote his report. When he was asked why he had gone to Sakhalin he answered, "My personal reasons for this journey are of no consequence."

The strictness that Chekhov exerted to maintain his privacy, not only from the public but also from friends and even his wife, characterizes the method of his work as a fiction writer and dramatist. Although his own life, as that of others, served as material, he completely refrained from making personal revelations. Just as he observed that there is no fourth wall to the stage, so his books were written not for the sake of the writer or the writing. Although there is no material other than life, it cannot simply be taken over as it is. It has to be dealt with and newly constructed—composed, in the true sense of the word. And so a new structure emerges—made and planned according to its own laws (such laws as balance, rhythm, conciseness, and control) that are not applicable to life—and this structure is a work of art. It will speak to the audience, which will judge it not by its form but its content. Chekhov's strict objectivity resembles that of a legal investigation. "The judgment is up to the jury" was one of his favorite sayings; his jury, of course, was the audience. For him, objective truth embraced justice.

Chekhov was searching for "the art of the quiet truth." Unlike Brecht, he believed that truth does not have to be made "conspicuous" in order to be perceived by the audience. To make it so would have struck Chekhov as manipulation. Unlike Brecht, he did not want to divorce emotion from the impact of truth; instead he sought to provoke it. After his return from Sakhalin, he said that he knew now with certainty that sermonizing was useless. What was needed was to present to the public the conditions as they really were—to evoke emotion, horror, indignation, and anger, and to move people to reflection. The truth, as Chekhov sought it out and presented it, is a kind of unmasking.

In the process by which Chekhov transformed his material into art, the truth is concentrated and hardened. All that is superfluous is sloughed off, and what is left is truly significant, right, and just. When all that is superfluous is removed, the foreground is cleared, and the audience can perceive "what is behind it" (and this Brecht also wanted to expose). In Chekhov's work, the truth in the background is always maintained in a quiet, low key. If it is made loud and "conspicuous," something important is lost: its enigmatic quality. Only where the truth remains quiet will it remain enigmatic and in the background. It is the possibility of its being perceived, not the volume, that must be increased.

The most serious misunderstanding of Chekhov's work was and still is caused by the confusion between "quietness" of truth and "quietness" of mood. Elements of mood, wherever called for in the plays, have dramatic significance. They may serve, for example, to create contrast or, as they frequently do, to provide a nuance of irony. Chekhov abhorred tearfulness and sentimentality. "You are colder toward people than the devil himself," Gorky once wrote to him. Chekhov's plays become falsified and distorted when they are swathed in veils of mournfulness, melancholy, and morbidity. Their true quality grows out of silence, and this silence begins where talk ends, when the surface becomes transparent and reveals the truth that lies behind it. Chekhov does not create impressions that lull the audience to drowse in a haze of sentimentality, preventing reflection and thought. He wants to communicate a distillation of truth that has to be acted out and put across between and beyond the lines, be it only through motionless and silent concentration of the power of imagination upon that which is to be imagined.

Chekhov's theater can be compared to a scientific experiment. The result is either accurate or wrong. It was and still is hard to learn this art of the quiet truth; we have only just begun to learn it.

ANTON CHEKHOV:
A BIOGRAPHICAL ESSAY

Anton Chekhov was born on January 29, 1860, in Taganrog, a mercantile city and a port on the northeastern shore of the Sea of Azov, which is an extension of the Black Sea. He grew up in the city's poor neighborhood, in a one-story house on a dirty street. On rainy days, one waded through mud. There was a small store in the house, and a tavern in the cellar. They were run by his father, a shopkeeper merchant in the lowest stratum of the petty bourgeoisie, who had been born a serf. Anton's capable grandfather, who was now the manager of a count's country estates, had saved enough money by 1841 to buy freedom for himself and his three sons. He had paid 300 rubles for the freedom of each.

When Anton was born, the system of serf ownership still existed in Russia. When it was abolished, he was one year old. The country was then ruled by Czar Alexander II, who was determined to bring at least a ray of light into the darkness of the anachronistic, medieval conditions that prevailed in Russia.

But the new freedom existed almost solely on paper. Although the peasants could no longer be sold, gambled away, or used as collateral by the great landowners, they still owned nothing. The earth they tilled belonged to their masters, and the unfortunate became further enslaved through debts. Thus the peasants, about eighty percent of the population, vegetated in ignorance, laziness, and drunkenness. As has happened throughout the ages, hunger and oppression were inciting revolts. By 1860 they had grown more intense. They now were led by university students, whose numbers were constantly increasing because of the advance of science and technology. Although the cruel "Third Department," the secret police, usually managed to destroy the rebels' hideouts and to torture, execute, or deport those who were arrested, rebellion was becoming more and more organized and the teachings of radicals and anarchists continued to spread among secondary-school and university students. In 1861, Bakunin went into permanent exile. The intelligence of the police state was, however, far from alert: in 1872 Karl Marx's *Kapital* was published in Russian translation, uncensored. It seems that the feudal system, now driven against the wall, was accelerating the people's hatred of capitalism. The Czar, for instance, was much amused by Gogol's *Government Inspector*, because it satirized civil servants, whose corruptness was well-known and hateful to him.

The medievalism of the national conditions were equalled by those inside the Chekhov home. Life behind the little store was, one may say, "under patriarchal rule"—it was a dog's life. The father was a tyrant who literally ruled with a knout. Later, Anton wrote to one of his two older brothers:

I beg you to remember that despotism and lies destroyed your mother's youth. Despotism and lies have spoiled our youth to such a degree that it is loathsome and terrible to recall it. Remember the fear and revulsion we felt every time Father threw his indignant and furious tantrums at the dinner table because the soup was too salty, reviling and insulting our mother as if she were a dim-witted imbecile.

Pavel Chekhov made his children toil in the shop, so that he could devote himself to higher pursuits and rise above the family's dingy everyday life. Above all, he was religious. He painted icons and led the church choir, while Anton and his older brothers worked in the store and in the tavern until nearly midnight. At dawn they were roused out of bed to serve in the church—to ring the church bells and sing hymns. "I no longer have religion," Anton admitted later. "You know, when my two brothers and I sang in church, when we chanted the trio 'He Shall Grow Better,' or 'The Voice of the Archangel,' everyone looked at us, moved by emotion. But we felt like little slave laborers."

The upper class of the city consisted of Greeks, who were shipowners and export merchants. One looked up with envy to these grand gentlemen and fine ladies. The pretentious father, instead of tending to his businesses, dreamed of his family's social ascent. He sent his three oldest sons to the school of the rich, the preparatory school attended by Greek boys, but this was a fiasco. The municipal preparatory school, which they attended later, was also remembered with bitterness by Anton. Most of the teachers were incompetent, and their methods of instruction stupid. Latin and Greek were crammed into the children in so humdrum a way that for all his life Anton had no taste for the literature of these languages.

We can see young Anton, in his student's uniform and cap, rushing through the streets; from school to the store, from the store to church, from church to the store. Or we see him, sleepy-eyed, serving behind the bar in the tavern among brawling drunks. At the age of fifteen he had an attack of pleurisy.

One year after Anton's first pleurisy attack his father went bankrupt. He had gotten into debt in order to move into a new house on a better street. A branch store (where Anton and his brothers worked behind the counter), near the newly constructed railroad station, was a failure. Though other townspeople were making profits, Pavel Chekhov no longer could pay his debts. Although the liberalizing Alexander II had introduced court reforms (floggings, except for convicts, were no longer decreed), the laws were still harsh. Those who could not pay their debts were thrown into prison. Pavel Chekhov escaped this fate by fleeing from the city, to Moscow, with part of his family. Because the Chekhovs feared they might be recognized in the Taganrog station, they took the train in the next town. The mother and the two youngest children, Masha and Michael, followed later, and only Anton stayed behind in Taganrog. He had received a scholarship, and had also begun to do some tutoring. The few rubles he earned even enabled him to send some money to his parents.

From there Anton received only letters of woe. The Chekhovs had fallen on hard times and were barely surviving in basements in the slums. Pavel Chekhov rarely found work, and the two oldest sons, Alexander and Nicholas, had left home. One of them was a student at the university and a journalist; the other, an art student at the academy. From time to time, whenever they had a few rubles to spare, they came to visit their family.

At the time, there were only four cities in Russia that had more than 100,000 inhabitants: Saint Petersburg, Moscow, Warsaw, and Odessa. After the emancipation of the serfs, however, the cities began to grow; to be more correct, the slums had swelled to an unhealthy size. The workers in the factories were no less exploited than the peasants who toiled on the land. In the slums ruled hunger, drunkenness, and vice. Pavel Chekhov, who had hoped to earn enough money in the big city to return in triumph to Taganrog, joined the ranks of the proletariat.

A year after the family's departure Anton had saved enough money to visit his family in Moscow. When he arrived, he was shocked. The family was living in a basement in the Grachevka, the district of the whorehouses. Through the windows one could see the feet of the passers-by. The mother toiled, dressed in a worn-out man's overcoat. The rest of the family sat around the table, on which the bottles stood as usual, while Pavel Chekhov made big speeches. But when the meager soup was served, steaming in the tureen, "we were as happy as never before."

In 1879, in Taganrog, Anton passed his university entrance examination. He then went to Moscow to join his family permanently. He arrived with a small sum of savings and with iron determination to improve their miserable lot.

Even the darkest youth has moments of light. Anton Chekhov was given neither to melancholy nor to dreaming. He had the mercurial temperament of the southern Russian; he loved gaiety, enjoyed jokes, and took the lead in many a boyish prank. He faced his tyrannical father with a stubborn defiance, which his submissive mother would complain about. Early in his life it was evident that Anton had a talent with which he delighted both his peers and the adults—a talent for inventing amusing stories. When he wrote them down in his school notebooks, in order to read them aloud to his schoolmates, his teachers found out about them, and, to his surprise, they did not scold him but laughed. He read his stories with such expressive miming that his schoolmates and teachers would ask him to rework them into plays, so that they could be acted out.

This would hardly have been possible had Anton not, together with his best friend, transgressed school rules by staying out late evening after evening. The two scraped together their kopecks to buy their regular seats in the balcony of the local theater. To escape the watchful eyes of the school inspector, they wore dark glasses and, for good measure, carried false beards in their coat pockets. They found the stage more exciting than anything in the world. They attended operettas, especially those of Offenbach, and they heard the voice of the great prima donna Lucca. They saw plays by Gogol, Griboedov, Ostrovsky, even Shakespeare—whatever was presented by the touring troupes. (The greatest success in those years, by the way, was a dramatization of *Uncle Tom's Cabin*.) Soon the boys found their way backstage. They made the acquaintance of a young comedian whom they were to know for a long time: it was Solovtsov, for whom Anton, ten years later, was to write his farce *The Bear*. Vishnevsky, Anton's friend and companion, later was to become an actor in Moscow.

Theater fever was rampant among the young students in Taganrog! In the salons of Anton's more affluent schoolmates, amateur performances were arranged. Anton, with great success, played the mayor in Gogol's *Government Inspector*. Yet he delighted his audience still more with his own improvisations, and most with his imitations. When he imitated priests and teachers, the spectators shook with laughter. The talent for satire was in his blood—a Russian tradition. At the time, of course, he was reading the then famous satirist, Saltykov-Shchedrin.

An interesting observation was recorded by a witness to these early theatrical exploits: Anton himself was not much given to laughter, though he never tired of amusing his audience. He amused them with material taken from the experiences of his own life —which were also the experiences of his audience. He literally took from "the fullness of life" and fashioned out of it his stories and jests. His imagination was always alert, ready to be inspired by people and objects alike. Once, as an acquaintance reported, he sat around a table with a group of people, most of them literati and journalists. One of them sighed and complained how hard it was to find material to write about. Astonished, Chekhov exclaimed, "What, no material? Here is an ashtray—tomorrow you'll have a story about it!"

What one usually calls inspirations were, in Chekhov's case, memories, which became the bases for his compositions. A wealth of possibilities would come to his mind while his imagination fed on his experiences and memories. And all his life he was inspired by the wish to amuse others.

His wife told friends that on the night he lay dying, he made her laugh with an improvised story. As she sat at his bedside, he conjured up a scene in an elegant hotel in a fashionable resort, full of fat bankers and red-cheeked Germans and Americans, just returning from the day's excursions, and all looking forward to a great meal. They are told that the cook has run away—there is shock, indignation, and outrage.

Did the young Anton view himself as the clown of the society he amused? No, he did not suffer from resentments and complexes. His self-confidence was strengthened by his well-handled early independence. Besides, he did not have the look of a loser who invites contemptuous treatment. He was strikingly handsome, slim and tall, with brown, wavy hair and sparkling eyes. There was no trace of the melancholy that later was to be ascribed to him because some people saw part of his literary work as an expression of his nature or were misled by the signs of his illness. Anton's demeanor was one of precocious maturity and manliness. Early and always, there were girls in his life. A sentence in an autobiographical sketch he composed for a journalist reads, "At the age of thirteen, I was introduced to the mysteries of love." The friends of his youth all agree that his relationships with women were pleasant and cheerful.

One of the joys of Anton's young days were hikes in the countryside. Nature was never to evoke in Chekhov romantic sentiment. He loved nature and described it with meticulous accuracy. He disliked gushing, flowery metaphors. He once said that he had found the best description of nature he had ever read in a schoolboy's composition that stated, "The sea is big." "Nature," he said later, "is an excellent sedative; it makes us indifferent. Only when one is capable of distance and indifference can one see clearly and judge justly." This kind of "indifference," which of course is something other than the indifference that critics later accused him of, was characteristic of Chekhov. Nature helped him gain the distance he yearned to put between himself and all things and human beings.

In the days of his youth, nature also evoked something else—a feeling of freedom. Out in the countryside he could escape from misery. He loved not merely nature, but also country life; it is no coincidence that he wrote about it in most of his plays. As a boy, he was happy when he was sent to visit his grandfather. On these visits he learned about the milieu of the landowners' country houses, which later he was so often to present in his plays. On a few occasions, he spent vacations on the estates of the families of schoolmates, some of them wealthy, others not. A visit to the Ukrainian steppes left so deep an impression that he recorded it later in *The Steppe*, a masterpiece. (Before writing it, however, he made a second journey into that region to check the accuracy of his impressions and reminiscences of the boy who was to be one of the major characters of the story.)

When the nineteen-year-old Chekhov arrived in Moscow, to take up his medical studies and lead his family out of their misery, the horizon of the world he was to draw upon in his fiction and plays was already set; he was never to step beyond it. This world was Russia, its cities and its countryside, its misery, its people. It was also love, writing, the theater. Science was to be added, but that addition, too, had already been decided upon.

Being a doctor was, relatively, free and safe in this medieval country whose period of liberalization, skimpy as it was, was about to give way to darkest reaction. During Chekhov's second year in Moscow, in 1881, the "good Czar," Alexander II, was assassinated by terrorists. Now the regime of

Alexander III began, with mass arrests and deportations. It also provided the most direct possibility of
aiding the suffering, which Chekhov, without stopping to talk about it, was to do until the very end of
his life. In addition, this profession provided the
best opportunity for ascertaining the truth about life
and men, for studying and defining it. The scientific
age indeed had begun as the age of the natural sci-
ences. The method of Flaubert (who died in 1880)
was to change the style of literature. For the theater,
an approach in a similar spirit had been created by
Georg Büchner (1813–37), a doctor whose dramas
were unknown to his own time.

Surely there is only one explanation of the remarkable and curious fact that Chekhov, who made
five extensive journeys abroad, wrote about nothing
but Russia, Russians, and Russian life. He was not
even remotely involved with Slavophilism. And he
had no connection with "populism" (the movement
of the Narodniks), which the liberals were talking
about at the time—going to the countryside, trying
to awaken the peasants, for they were the "true
Russia." The fact that he wrote so exclusively about
Russia can only be explained by the recognition that
he wrote only about what he understood and knew. It
is his accuracy (according to Ehrenburg) that makes
Chekhov an author of the twentieth century.

I cannot close these pages about Chekhov's youth
without quoting the following selection from a letter
he wrote to Suvorin, his publisher and friend:

> What the writers who come from the aristoc-
> racy receive free, the intellectuals from the
> lower classes have to buy dear at the cost of
> their youth.—Think of writing a story about a
> young man, the son of a serf, a store clerk,

choir singer, gymnasium and later university
student. A boy brought up to revere the class
structure of the society, to kiss the hand of
priests, to admire foreign ideas. A boy who has
to be thankful for every piece of bread he eats,
who is often beaten, who goes to school without
overshoes. A boy who torments himself and who
tortures animals; who plays the hypocrite before God and men just out of the conviction of
his own worthlessness. Think of writing about
how this young man, drop by drop, squeezes the
slave out of himself. How he wakes up one
beautiful morning and feels that in his veins
no longer flows the blood of a serf, but real
blood—the blood of a human being.

2.

Now Chekhov was to live through ten wretched,
desperate, restless years, years in which he experienced undreamed-of success and social ascent. They
were to end with fame though not happiness. In fact
they were to end with the opposite—a radical break
with everything that had been stable until then. Then,
his departure for Sakhalin, the island of the damned.
Chekhov, the medical student, began to write.
Alexander, his oldest brother, a muddlehead who
was always involved in affairs with women, had
some contact with several editors on small papers
and periodicals who occasionally accepted one of
his manuscripts. While still living in Taganrog,
Chekhov had sent him some stories, a few of which
were printed. Now writing became a source of income. Chekhov wrote to earn his living, to pay for
his tuition, to support his family—apparently for no
other reason. He met with some success, and soon he

no longer needed his mentor, Alexander. His work pleased the editors of Moscow's humorous publications and their readers. One of his pseudonyms became well-known: Chekonte. His aim was to be amusing, and to achieve this was no problem for him. His head was always full of amusing story ideas. And now that he lived in the big city, his subject range became broader.

Chekhov was not a stay-at-home loner. The shabby apartment, in which he and his family lived on the rubles he earned with his writing, a kopeck per line, was always full of guests. Along with the students there were artists from the circle of his unfortunate brother Nicholas.

Nicholas, a bohemian and heavy drinker, would be out of touch with the family for long periods. From time to time, ragged and ill, he would turn up again. Chekhov loved Nicholas very much and thought his paintings extraordinary. He died at the age of thirty-two devoured by consumption.

Anton befriended a group of actors and actresses, and it is said that he had an affair with one of the young women, a dancer. With his new companions he went on the town. They visited bars and the apartments of cultured people and went to the theater. In these years he became familiar with poverty and wretchedness in places the bourgeois calls dens of iniquity and hotbeds of crime. Nothing human was alien to Chekhov; everywhere he found material for both his professions—medicine and literature.

In the daytime he studied, in the evenings he went out, at night he wrote. That was his life style during those years. He pursued his medical studies with great seriousness, not just because it was necessary that he finish them as soon as possible but because he was passionately interested in the subject—the body, life, human beings. "I don't want to be one of the people who have a negative attitude toward science," he said. He also said, "I want to belong among those who depend solely on their own research and insight into everything."

The point at which science tears away one's blinders and affords a clear view of life is quickly reached: what hunger and privation have brought about, the physician usually cannot cure. The students who had come to this realization were no longer satisfied with studying and having a good time. The university was gripped by unrest. Discussions were held in secret, and there was talk of revolt against the government. All these young people were haunted by what was to be the great question of the coming decades: Reform? Or more of the old reign of terror?

The populist movement of the Narodniks gained ground among the intelligentsia. Chekhov did not participate in this movement; he found it too romantic for his taste. Neither did he join the radicals; he did not think much of assassinations. In 1881, when he was in his sixth semester, the student rebellion broke loose. The signal was the assassination of Alexander II. But this also was a signal for the reaction. The liberalizing Alexander II was now succeeded by Alexander III, a brutal oppressor. Upon his orders the unrest was put down with draconic severity. The Cossacks, brought in to intervene, cruelly put down the rebellion. There were mass arrests and mass deportations. Chekhov had to say farewell to many a fellow student; many were sent to Siberia. "Russia is becoming one single, enormous prison camp," wrote Elsa Triolet. There was an atmosphere of funereal quiet. The populist movement, too, came to an end. The peasants were pushed back into their old state of misery. And the miserably paid average workday for the industrial worker now consisted of eleven and a half hours.

As Chekhov began his last semester at medical school, he wrote:

> In addition to the examinations, there is the dissection of cadavers. There is the clinical work, with its unavoidable load of case records and hospital visits. I work and work, and begin to feel physical weakness. My memory is becoming bad, lazy. The literature stinks of schnapps. I have fears that I won't pass. . . .

Chekhov did not mention here that he also was writing every day; every week he submitted one or two stories. He had commissions for reportage, for accounts of courtroom cases. And he was constantly coughing up blood and running a temperature. He was far from thinking of his writing as literature. Yet, now he made his first contact with a serious journal, *Fragments*, which was published in Saint Petersburg. Its editor, Leykin, asked him to become a regular contributor. At this time Chekhov wrote that a good story must contain, besides an interesting plot, an "effective note of protest." Most of the pieces he wrote in this period were satirical, some so aggressively so that they did not pass the censor. He liked to choose themes on the borderline of what could be printed. As the censors served the upper crust of the ruling class, they let much go by that attacked the middle class, that satirized civil servants and police. For the censors were aware that such stories amused the fine gentlemen and ladies of high society. One of the characters Chekhov invented in this period, Sergeant Prishibeyev, gained such popularity that his name entered the Russian language.

Under the pseudonym Ulysses, Chekhov wrote "Fragments from Moscow Life" for the Saint Petersburg *Fragments*. One day, in a café frequented by literati, he overheard a spirited conversation at a neighboring table. One of the talkers laughingly called the mysterious Ulysses "a talented pig." In 1884, his story *A Young Man* created a sensation because of the "candor" with which it spoke of "the falling of the ruble and the corruption of public servants in high places." The name Chekonte became well-known. In 1883, under this pseudonym, 112 of Chekhov's stories and reportage pieces were published.

We should not forget under what circumstances these manuscripts were written. In the summer, the student at least was able to take his table outside, into the fresh air; but in the winter he had to work at the table that stood in the family's living room. "I write under the most depressing conditions," Chekhov wrote at the time. "Through the door I hear the crying of the child of a relative who has come to visit us; my father is reading a story to my mother. And someone has turned on the gramophone and is listening to the music of *La Belle Hélène*. . . ."

He even had to share his bed at night with the relative mentioned here. And he shared the bedroom with his brothers. Yet, every ruble he earned went into the family till. The letters he wrote in this period are full of one continuing theme: money, and the need for money. He never had so much as a ten-ruble note in his pocket. As he no longer had the time to deliver his manuscripts himself to the editorial offices, Michael, one of his younger brothers, became his messenger. Michael also took over the most difficult task: fee-collecting. "At the

markable state of affluence, though the worries about
money were not yet over. The poor young boy had
become a medical doctor. And all he possessed he
had earned by his writing. As he reached this turning
point in his life, did his writing really have as little
meaning to him as he claimed?

In 1923, a hitherto unpublished play that we shall
call *Platonov* appeared in print. Platonov, the name
of the protagonist, is also the title of most of the
play's English translations. This play, which should
not be evaluated by its unsatisfactory adaptations,
was written in those early years in Moscow. For six
months, it is reported, he hardly wrote anything else.
For he needed this interval to think and work through
to a finish what had been on his mind for a long
time. Chekhov himself said that he visualized this
work as "an encyclopedia of Russian life"—an enormous task.

I shall speak more fully of *Platonov* in my discus-
sion of the plays, for I am convinced that, despite
the work's weaknesses, it deserves a place with *The
Sea Gull*, *The Three Sisters*, and *The Cherry Orchard*, and that, for instance, it surpasses *Ivanov*. At
the time it was written, there was nothing that could
be compared to it. This first undertaking of Chekhov
the dramatist has unbelievable originality, freshness,
and innovation. It testifies to Chekhov's outlook and
program, which he never changed, although the form
and design of this first experiment suffered from his
lack of experience, experience which he was to acquire
between the writing of *Platonov* and that of *The Sea
Gull*. Yet even the form of his plays was not to
change fundamentally, merely to become more clear
and purified.

Platonov was Chekhov's first literary work. He had

end of last year," Chekhov wrote in 1886, "I f
like a bone that's been thrown to the dogs."

In many ways the year 1886 was a turning poir
Chekhov now became a doctor of medicine. In t
country, where Ivan, the youngest and "most nc
mal" of the siblings, now worked as a teacher, Anto
treated his first private patients and also worked
the public hospital. Little is known about his pra
tice in Moscow, in the period that followed, exce
that it cost more money than it brought in. The mo
the income from his writing increased, the mo
patients he treated without charging a fee. One ca
imagine how quickly that became known. Often 1
could hardly handle his growing number of patient

With deep satisfaction Chekhov described tl
gradual improvement of his family's circumstance
After several moves he purchased a little house f
them in Sadovaya Street, a two-story brick buildir
with seven rooms. For the first time, he had his ov
study. He was happy finally to have space for h
library, which consisted of more than a thousar
books. His mother and his sister, with two maids
do the housework, were now free from domest
labors. Pavel Chekhov now gave up his poor job in
department store to enjoy his home and his servan
"Father and Mother have to eat," Chekhov used
say. Chekhov's only sister, Masha, who had receiv
a good education, was capable of giving him a go
deal of assistance. All through his life, she was to
a loyal helper. Brother Michael, now twenty yea
old, was studying law. At the same time, he was al
preparing himself for the task to which he w
destined—to be the biographer and literary execut
of his great older brother. And in the summer, it w
possible to rent a house in the country.

In these six years, Chekhov had achieved a

hardly been involved at all with the pieces he had written to earn money. The existence of this play and his great preoccupation with it disproves the always again repeated statement that only through the esteem of others did he come to recognize that he had more than an average knack for writing. His first play met with complete lack of understanding and sympathy. This was a great shock to him, perhaps the gravest in these ten years. It was to be followed by a second and similar one—the failure of a long novel on which he had worked for years. The novel met with the same fate as the play: he destroyed the manuscript. Nothing is left of the novel.

In June 1881, the student Anton Chekhov had come to the stage door of the Imperial Maly Theater with a parcel under his arm. He handed it to the doorman and asked that it be delivered to the celebrated actress Marya Yermolova. (Then twenty-nine years old, she was to die in 1928 as "an artist of the Soviet Peoples.") Had he met her? Did someone recommend him to her? We do not know. But what she meant to him and to his generation we have heard from Stanislavsky, who was three years younger than Chekhov.

> To us this name signified a whole epoch in the Russian theater. For our generation, she was the symbol of femininity, of beauty and strength, of vitality and verve, of sincere simplicity and modesty. . . . She had the body of a Venus and a deep, warm voice; she projected grace, harmony, and rhythm, even in scenes of chaos and violence. She also had incredible charm and stage personality, which turned even her flaws into virtues. . . .

The young Russians were not without means of comparison. That very year, as Chekhov reported in *Fragments*, the Moscow audience went wild over Sarah Bernhardt on tour. He himself missed in her what, evidently, Madame Yermolova possessed for him—"the flame." The only actress he was to admire more was Eleonora Duse, whom he was to see ten years later.

For days after submitting his manuscript Chekhov waited for an answer from Yermolova. Eventually, the mailman brought a package. We can imagine how Chekhov grabbed it from the mailman's hands and opened it, his heart beating wildly. It was the manuscript of the play. Nothing else. Not a word from Marya Yermolova. He probably destroyed the manuscript immediately because this finished copy was not seen again, though a heavily edited draft was found among his papers after his death. The next time he was to have a similar experience with another play at the same theater, he was already famous. That time he was to receive a note. The leading actor of the Maly Theater advised him to leave the theater alone —he had no talent for it.

It seems that Chekhov believed in the judgment of the theater people. Six years went by before the theater director Korsh, for whom Tolstoy also wrote a play, succeeded in convincing Chekhov of the opposite. The circumstances indicate that it must have been a kind of bet between them. Such plays as you want, I can write in no time, Chekhov may have said, before bringing the first draft of *Ivanov* to Korsh eleven days later. And it did grow into half a Chekhov work. During this period, he amused himself with writing one-acters. They meant as little to him as the stories he wrote for the humorous papers and journals, but they did prove, at least, that he did not suffer from lack of talent, despite the rejection of his plays by a star actor and actress.

The turning point arrived: in March 1886, Chekhov received a letter. It was from Grigorovich, the eminent storyteller, known as the founder of the Russian school of realism, whose name was mentioned with those of Tolstoy and Dostoyevsky. He was also honored by the official Russian establishment, having received the title of Actual Privy Councillor, and was considered one of the country's great men. "Unexpectedly, suddenly, like a *deus ex machina*," Chekhov wrote to a friend, "I received a letter from Grigorovich. . . . He is convinced that I really have talent. . . ."

In the meantime, two volumes of collected stories had appeared. The first volume, described as a collection of "theater stories," was entitled *Melpomene*. The second, *Motley Tales*, was described by Chekhov himself as a "mixed salad." Both consternation and joy are reflected in his answer to Grigorovich, who had warned him not to fritter away his talent:

> Your letter, my warmly admired bringer of glad tidings, has struck me like a thunderbolt. . . . It is as if I were intoxicated with joy. . . . In the five years I have been around the newspapers, I have come to accept the general view of my literary insignificance. . . . Until now my literary work has been done frivolously, carelessly, and without thoughtfulness. . . . And now, quite unexpectedly, comes your letter. Excuse the comparison, but it has affected me like a governor's order to leave town in twenty-four hours. That is, I suddenly feel the need to get out from where I am bogged down. . . .

Grigorovich, who could not have known Chekhov's circumstances, had written that Chekhov should starve rather than let himself be rushed for material by the newspapers. Chekhov answered, "I do not refuse to go hungry, I have suffered hunger before. . . . My whole hope belongs to the future! I am only twenty-six years old. Perhaps I shall manage to accomplish something, though time is passing so quickly."

Never did Chekhov dream that his short stories could be looked upon as literature. Now, suddenly, he heard himself called "the Russian Maupassant." He had achieved such virtuosity in the genre he was using that he could play with its forms without effort, and this now was noticed by the literati and critics. Grigorovich's letter had a revolutionary effect upon his consciousness.

Then, around that same time, Russia's most prominent publisher showed interest in him—Suvorin, an unusual man, an autodidact, who had worked his way up from the lowest strata of the society. Suvorin first achieved success as a writer, then, as a "lackey of the upper class," as Lenin called him. Later, rewarded with special subsidies, he became a millionaire. Suvorin seems to have been a fascinating, powerful personality. For a long time, Chekhov—who carried on a lengthy correspondence with Suvorin and traveled with him several times—considered him his best friend. But the shamelessly reactionary attitude of Suvorin's press during the Dreyfus affair was to bring about a serious break between the two men. But now, in 1886, Chekhov, who had just been honored by Grigorovich, became a contributor to Suvorin's publication, which was Russia's most influential newspaper.

Chekhov's income and status grew. On a visit to Saint Petersburg he was received with honors far beyond his expectations. But his financial worries were not yet over. "Yes, indeed, it is a joy to be a famous writer," he wrote. "I have to work from morning till night, yet show no profit for it. I don't have a kopeck. I don't know how Zola and Shchedrin manage. . . . I, anyhow, have less money than talent." Or: "As always, the firm of Dr. Chekhov is in financial crisis. If you won't lend me twenty-five or thirty rubles till the first of the month, you're a heartless crocodile." Suvorin lent him three hundred rubles, so he could take a trip to the south. Giving half of it to his family, he arranged for them to spend the summer on the country estate of one of his wealthy new acquaintances in Babkino, near Moscow. There they stayed in a little house by the river. He himself was being pampered by the owners, spending his time on literature and music. Tchaikovsky was one of the guests. Here Chekhov had a real desk: a dismantled sewing machine.

Now that he was "as popular as [Zola's] *Nana*," he took a trip to the South to revisit Taganrog, where he had spent his wretched youth. It was not merely a pleasure trip; he was working on a new "encyclopedia." It was to be called *The Steppe*. His objective was like the one he had in writing *Platonov*, but now he shaped his material into the genre that had brought him literary fame. It was to become a great story—one of his masterpieces. At the same time, he was living in the world of his novel. Again in Moscow, in the winter of 1888, he wrote, "Everything I have written so far is nonsense compared to what I want to write. . . . I don't like my success. I don't like anything I am writing now. . . . I need to be alone and to have some time to myself." That year the Imperial Academy honored him with the Pushkin Prize.

Thus approached the year 1889, marked by unprecedented severity. In it Chekhov was to be subjected to experiences that would lead to grave consequences. Looking back, one sees that the crisis could have been foreseen. From all directions, pressures were bearing down upon him.

The first was illness. It is said that Chekhov only late in his life came to realize the true nature of his symptoms. But this cannot be true. For these symptoms were so unmistakable that one did not have to be a physician to diagnose them. He coughed up blood, had subfebrile temperatures, headaches, blood in the stool—clear evidence of tuberculosis of the lung and the intestines. Dr. Chekhov pretended to his friends, and especially to his family, that it was all quite harmless. He did nothing to cure himself. How could he when he was so busily simulating health? Years later, when the attacks had become more and more terrifying, his condition became the subject of quarrels with his parents. Finally he had to give in; the family insisted that they all move to the country. Only after friends had to drag him to a hospital after witnessing a grave attack, did he consult his colleagues. From then on there was no more dissembling.

By April 1886, if not before, he must have known how things stood with him. At that time he became seriously ill after covering a trial because the reporter's desk, where he sat, was exposed to an icy draft. It is not easy to simulate health. Chekhov's skeptical sense of self-irony, his strong nerves, and his congenital need for discretion and privacy gave him the strength to accomplish it. One can imagine what went on in the mind of this taciturn, reserved man after he realized that he did not have long to live. With grim laughter he told his friends of an experience he had when he and the poet Leskov had just become friends. Interested in spiritualism, Chekhov and Leskov attended a séance together. There the spirit of the recently deceased Turgenev appeared to announce to Chekhov, "You will die young."

Chekhov was not a man to fear death; he accepted it as a fact. He seems to have been far more disturbed by his frustration with the theater. Before he had recuperated from the rejection of *Platonov*, he had to experience a second fiasco. *Ivanov*—the play he had written with almost cynical haste to show the commercial theater people that he could manufacture a play for them to order—incited an unprecedented, scandalous riot at its premiere in the Korsh Theater. During the performance, part of the audience drowned out the lines with shouts and screams. Chekhov was hailed with laughter and catcalls. At the end, the audience came to blows, and the brawl looked so dangerous that the police had to be called in to clear the theater. Chekhov reported later that most of the actors had been drunk. He also said that the prompter's voice was often more audible than that of the actors, none of whom had known their lines. But Chekhov must also have been aware of the weakness of this first, quickly written version. After he had finished the second version he said it had so taken hold of him that he "had lost all sense of time and believed he was going mad."

Originally, *Ivanov* was conceived as a slick play, but as Chekhov proceeded with his writing it became a true Chekhov work. Yet its freshness and originality, qualities that had been evident in the *Platonov* project, struck the audience, used to more ordinary fare, as strange. His masterpiece *The Sea Gull* was to fare no better. Such innovation could only become acceptable in time, as the plays continued to be performed. A year after the Korsh Theater scandal, the revised version of *Ivanov* was a sensational success in Saint Petersburg.

And yet, no one knew better than Chekhov the weakness of *Ivanov*, which was beyond revision. He knew he had made a compromise.

Again, he set himself to work. Possibly, at that time, Stanislavsky's founding of the Moscow Society for Art and Literature—which demanded a new and modern kind of drama—led Chekhov to have greater expectations than he admitted to himself and to his friends. For almost a full year, he worked on a curious and remarkable play, which seemed to just flow out of his pen—*The Wood Demon*. (The Russian title, *Leshy*, sounds less romantic, so the French title, *Le Sauvage*, may be more acceptable than the English title, though this, too, only vaguely suggests the nature of the protagonist.) We will examine the play later, in connection with *Uncle Vanya*, in which some of the dialogue and several of the characters reappeared ten years later. *The Wood Demon* again was a compromise, though of a different kind than *Ivanov*. It was a compromise with what then was called "Tolstoyism." Chekhov, by then a famous writer, submitted the manuscript to the Imperial Theater. He was taken aback when the program committee, which consisted of a number of notable figures (among them Grigorovich), called the play, not without respect, "an excellent dramatized story but not drama." The committee asked for changes, which they believed would heighten the play's effectiveness on the stage. Chekhov withdrew the work and submitted it to one of Moscow's many private theaters. There it was performed, on December 27, 1889—and was a miserable failure. Chekhov's reaction was fitting to that year of crises: he would not permit publication or further performances of the play. (It was not to be published until after Chekhov's death.) This was not the only disappointment of that year; a short time ago, he had burned the manuscript of his novel.

That June, his favorite brother, Nicholas, the painter, died of the same disease that was consuming Chekhov. Kolya had returned from one of his wild bohemian bouts sick unto death; despite all medical care and attention, he could not be saved. He was only thirty-two years old.

An unhappy love affair also contributed to the difficulties of that year. Lydia Avilova, a young writer, has described it herself, as she saw it. She was then twenty-five years old, married, and the mother of a little boy. Called "the beautiful Flora," she was a lady of society, and her husband was one of Chekhov's friends. "Friendship stands higher than love," Chekhov said. He withdrew, and avoided her for years.

But an additional, overpowering force was pulling at him, one that led to a point where there was no way out. We have mentioned "Tolstoyism." Chekhov, looking back, was to write later:

> I was strongly moved by Tolstoy's philosophy. It dominated my thoughts for six or seven years. It was not his major theses that affected me, I had been acquainted with them before. It was Tolstoy's way of expressing himself, his thoughtfulness—and probably a kind of hypnosis.

It must have been a kind of obsession. Ever since people had impressed upon him his literary importance, Chekhov was obsessed with the thought that everything he was writing should have a deeper meaning. In 1886, Tolstoy published an alarming essay entitled, *What Then Must We Do?* It proclaimed his "conversion." He now preached a new, true Christianity: thou shalt not own anything; thou shalt not use force and violence; thou shalt not judge others. This teaching of love was an answer to the unbearable condition of the world. Tolstoy himself was to bear the last consequence of these tenets shortly before his death. But he was already wearing the peasant's blouse. He stepped in wherever there was the most glaring misery, founding shelters to feed the hungry and appealing to the conscience of the rich. His peasant drama *The Power of Darkness* moved many of his contemporaries, although its performance was prohibited in Russia. That he went unscathed, despite his doctrine of nonviolence—which meant that he urged men to refuse to do military service—was due to Tolstoy's world fame. One let him preach.

Chekhov, who had a plan for the theater, could not ignore *The Power of Darkness*. He destroyed the manuscript of his ambitious novel when Tolstoy's *Kreutzer Sonata* appeared. The challenging figure of the great Tolstoy would not let him go. No one knew more of the injustice among men than the son of a serf who was experiencing the results of hunger and deprivation in his own body. Indeed, the physician knew more about this matter than the Count. And Chekhov, as he said later, was repelled by Tolstoy's demeanor of the prophet. Although he would have said that he loved no human being more than he loved Tolstoy, he was not blind to the weaknesses of Tolstoy the man and the inhumanity of part of his philosophy. Yet, despite this, it was Tolstoy's influence that changed Chekhov's literary work, and not necessarily to its advantage, as is demonstrated in *The Wood Demon*. In *Platonov*, too, the characters express reflections about God, the world, and the times; these are, however, the reflections of very particular characters. But now, under the influence of Tolstoy, ideas have pervaded Chekhov's dialogue in a different way.

Yet Chekhov felt that all this philosophizing might lead him astray. He began to recognize that, to the question *What Then Must We Do?*, he could not reply as Tolstoy had done. He had to find his own answer. And the conditions of the times demanded an answer. Nonviolence—that was a possibility; terrorism, which leads to revolution, was another. But Chekhov was not born to be either a prophet or an assassin. He was a physician and a writer. What could a doctor do? What could a writer do?

February 1888. I am living through a crisis. If I don't find the take-off point, it will go downward with me.

October 1888. Our misfortune is not that we hate our enemies, of which we do not have many, but that we do not have enough love for our fellowmen, of which there are as many as the grains of sand by the sea.

May 1889. Suddenly it does not interest me any more to see my stories in print. Criticism, literary conversations, talk, successes, failures, fees, all are no longer of any concern to me. In one sentence: they have become meaningless to me. I now feel like a downright fool. Somehow, things have come to a standstill for me. It is because I have come to an impasse in my personal life. I am not disappointed, I am not tired, not

melancholic—it is just that everything suddenly
has become less interesting. I must try to find
some incentive, to get off the ground.

December 1889. Sketches and feuilletons, foolish bits, vaudevilles, boring stories, a lot of mis-
takes and nonsense, pounds of manuscript paper,
a price from the academy, a biography of Potemkin—and among all this not one line that I consider of any literary value. A lot of forced work,
but not a moment of serious effort. I long to hide
away somewhere for five years, and to occupy
myself with hard and serious work.

By the end of the year 1889 he had found an answer: it was to go to Sakhalin.

March 1890. I go with the deep conviction
that my journey will not be a valuable contribution either to literature or to science. For that I
have neither enough background nor knowledge,
time, or ambition. . . . I want to write at least a
hundred or two hundred pages, and so make
some restitution to medicine, toward which, as
you know, I've behaved like a swine. . . . Even if
the journey has nothing to offer, should there not
be two or three days that I shall remember all
my life? . . . Sakhalin can be of no use and no
interest only to a society that banishes to it
thousands of human beings. . . . Sakhalin is a
place of unbearable suffering. . . . I regret that I'm
not sentimental; otherwise I would say that we
should pilgrimage to places like Sakhalin, as the
Turks go to Mecca. From the books I have read
and am still reading I take it that we let millions
of people rot in jails, rot for nothing, without

thought or reflection, barbarically. We have chased human beings, in chains, in bitter cold, for tens of thousands of miles, have infected them with syphilis, have corrupted them morally, have increased the number of criminals—and all this we blame on the red-nosed prison guards. The whole of civilized Europe knows that it's all of us, not the prison guards, who are guilty. But that doesn't trouble us, it is uninteresting. . . . No, I assure you, Sakhalin is necessary, and interesting. It is a pity that it is only I who is going there, not someone who would understand the conditions better than I do and is better equipped to publicize them and to motivate public interest in them. My personal reasons for going there really are of no consequence.

Chekhov did not begin his journey with the grim attitude of a martyr. Although he felt as if he were going to war, he observed that he was not facing personal danger—except for a toothache he was sure to get. As soon as he made his decision to go to Sakhalin, his personal crisis was over and he plunged into plans and preparations. For three months, before setting out, he devoted himself to the study of documents, reports, and official data. And he obtained interviews with members of the imperial prison administration.

He did not receive official support for his project to examine the hygienic and sanitary conditions of the prisoners; but he was promised that he would be free to proceed. Yet, a secret official telegram preceded him, asking that the governor not permit him to see the political prisoners. Despite this, he was to find a surprising amount of understanding among the

higher civil servants on the island. When people
learned what he was going to do, it created a stir.
But he rejected all interpretations of his decision. "I
want to erase a year or a year and a half from my life.
I am not traveling to collect observations and impressions for literary use, but only in order to live differently for half a year than I have lived until now."

His leave-taking was gay. A woman friend accompanied him on the steamboat journey up the Volga,
to Perm. He traveled on by railroad, then, for 4,000
kilometers, by stagecoach, through the Taiga and on
to Lake Baikal. He continued by boat, and then again
by coach. Often, Siberia was like a nightmare.
Though it was May, it was still winter, and Chekhov
shivered in the bitter cold and coughed up blood. For
a week he stayed in Irkutsk, where he felt well and
happy. Finally, after traveling for two and a half
months, he reached Nikolayevsk at the sea. On July
11, 1890, he arrived at Sakhalin.

Now his work began. He rose every morning at
five o'clock and went to bed late at night. He adhered
to a well-prepared work plan. As soon as he had completed an investigation, he integrated the data into
his statistical material. He visited every camp, every
village.

The convicts were divided into various divisions.
Some of them had to bear heavy chains on their feet.
A few lived as "free settlers," most of them in
wretched huts. The misery in the women's camp was
indescribable. The women were being "dealt out—
shared." Almost every night someone attempted to
escape. The punishment was barbaric. "I have been
present at a flogging. Afterward, for three or four
nights, I dreamed of the hangman and of the loathsome block." Two months he spent in the central part

of the island, one month in the south. Often the climate was murderous. "At the end, my nerves were a frazzle." But he had collected enough material for "at least three dissertations."

The result: Sakhalin disproved Tolstoy's thesis of nonviolence. Chekhov felt that one must describe the conditions as they were and force the people to face them and to respond. He became convinced that sermons are useless, and that one should write at the dictation of emotion and reality.

"For two months I worked strenuously, not sparing myself in any way. In the third month I began to weaken, because of the bitterness. . . ."

On his return journey he saw Hong Kong, Singapore, Ceylon ("the paradise"), and the Red Sea. "How beautiful is the Lord's world! Only one thing is not good: we."

The book that described the "Remembrances of Hell" is a scientific report. Yet it moved his contemporaries. Even the government was roused sufficiently to send a commission of inquiry to the island. Though some of the worst abuses were abolished, no sweeping reform was instituted.

Now Chekhov had only thirteen years left to live. These were the years in which he was to create his major works and in which his fame and affluence were to grow. And these also were the years in which the course of his illness would progress. He dined with Tchaikovsky, for whom he was to write a libretto. Tolstoy asked that he come and visit him in Yasnaya Polyana: the old man was deeply moved by the meeting, for he was very fond of Chekhov. Gorky (whom Chekhov later introduced to Tolstoy) related how Chekhov reacted when Tolstoy, who was not reticent with criticism of Chekhov, showered him with praise after reading one of his stories. Gorky reported that Chekhov, after a long silence, said, uneasily, "There are many printer's errors in it."

These were happy days. In 1891, Chekhov treated himself to a journey through Europe. He visited Vienna, Venice and Rome, Nice and Paris. From Vienna he wrote, "It seems strange that one can read everything and about everything, and can talk about whatever one wishes to." He was enchanted by the beauty of these cities, but soon he grew tired. In Paris all the streets were full of the military—the result of the May riots.

When he was home again—after an altercation with his family, from whom he could no longer hide the fact of his illness—he finally decided to move to the country. For 13,000 rubles, two-thirds of which was borrowed, he bought an estate in Melikhovo— 232 hectares of land, 100 hectares of forest. The son of the serf was now a landowner. Father, mother, and sister moved into the manor house. In the cherry orchard he had a little studio built for himself. (Here he was to write *The Sea Gull*.) There was "a park; great trees, a long avenue bordered with lindens, a lake." He loved to go fishing, to plant shrubs, to tend the trees. "Our mother went to church today in her own carriage, and our father fell from the sled because the horses were so frisky." He told a visitor that he longed for the day when he no longer would have to write. Then he would devote himself to gardening. He wrote to Suvorin:

"My soul is withering away because I have to write for money. . . . I don't value what I write . . . I am glad that I have my medical profession, which I do not practice for the sake of money. One should bathe in sulphuric acid, shed one's skin, and then grow a new one." He used to say that medicine was his legal wife, literature his mistress—"When I'm tired of the one, I spend the night with the other." And the peasants came running to the doctor who didn't take any money.

In 1891 and 1892 there was a famine and an epidemic of cholera. Now Dr. Chekhov was appointed district doctor. While Tolstoy was founding shelters, Chekhov was rushing from one sickbed to the next.

> Death gathers in mankind. There is no time to write. Now all doctors are working, working furiously. At the fair of Nizhni Novgorod, miracles are performed that could move even a Tolstoy to respect medical science. . . . From August until October 10 I have entered in my card file 500 patients. In all, I must have examined 1,000. . . . This summer, life was hard, but it seems to me that I have spent no summer better. . . . The tragedies take place in peasant huts and out under the sky. The devil take the philosophy of the great ones of this world!

Now he was through with Tolstoyism.

In the winter, again in Moscow, Chekhov inspected factories and their sanitary facilities. (And Thomas Mann was convinced that Chekhov "had no relationship to the working class"!) During this winter, his health deteriorated rapidly. For the first time he went to Yalta. The spring in the Crimea agreed with him. Then, on a second European journey, he went to the Riviera.

The death of Czar Alexander III, in 1894, led the Russian intelligentsia to wild hopes. But his successor, Nicholas II (who was to be shot in 1918 at Yekaterinburg) continued the reign of terror. The following summer, Chekhov was named school inspector for the district of his estate. During this period, he used his own funds to erect and support three schools. "I had three schools built, and they are said to be of model standard. . . . Two schools cost me 3000 rubles each, the third, smaller one, almost 2000 rubles." He tried to gain the support of the Czarina for the building of a children's day-care center on Sakhalin, but without success. Of a millionaire's wife, whom he had asked for 666 rubles for books for his schools, he reports: "her tongue got stuck to the roof of her mouth."

Now he began to work on *The Sea Gull.*

3.

Two events put a definite stamp upon Chekhov's last years. He had too little of what one calls a world view to relinquish all hope; but fate saw to it that his happy days never lasted long. He knew he was not to live long—and saw no chance for the production of his plays.

The first event, on October 17, 1896, was the fiasco at the premiere of *The Sea Gull.* In November 1895 he had, essentially, finished the play. Chekhov knew that with this work he had reached the goal he had set himself, and he believed that now the project he had begun with *Platonov* was ready for the stage. He was eager to do a reading of the play in Moscow. The audience gathered in the Korsh Theater, in the dressing room of the actress Javorskaya, with whom he then was having an affair. The reaction of the listeners hit him like blows. "My dear boy," said Korsh, "but this is not dramatic! You let your hero shoot himself backstage, and, before that, you don't even give him a chance for a monologue onstage?" Chekhov went home and put the manuscript into his desk.

The following January, the Imperial Alexander Theater in Saint Petersburg showed interest in the new Chekhov play. The management was prepared to accept his condition: the playwright's participation in rehearsals. In September, the casting of the roles was completed. When the rehearsals were about to begin, his illness erupted and he was confined to his bed. Only a week before opening night was he finally able to travel to Saint Petersburg. During one of the last rehearsals the actress playing Nina walked out. Fortunately, there was a substitute, who proved to be more than adequate. It was Vera Kommissarzhevskaya, who was soon to become one of the leading actresses of the Russian theater. At the dress rehearsal, she provided the only ray of hope.

Then came the evening of the catastrophe. During the first act, the play was drowned out by derisive laughter. Onstage, Nina lost her composure. During intermission, Chekhov sat in one of the dressing rooms. Actresses fluttered by; "officials" in uniform appeared backstage, and Chekhov had to listen to the whispers and giggling of the "parasites" (the visitors backstage). He did not return to the auditorium. After the last act, when it was quite clear that the play had flopped, he left the theater. Suvorin had invited the actors and some friends to the Romanov restaurant. Chekhov did not appear. His friends were worried and tried to look for him. It was two o'clock in the morning when he finally arrived at the restaurant. "Where have you been?" asked his friends. "I walked through the streets," was the answer. The next morning he took the train home. At the railway station he said to a friend who was seeing him off, "This is the end. I shall not write another play."

The critics demolished him. After five performances, the play closed. Chekhov wrote, "On October

17 it was not my play that experienced failure, but my very person. I have quieted down now; my mood is back to ordinary. But I cannot forget what has happened; just as I could not forget if someone, for instance, had thrashed me." And somewhat later: "Let's have no actors, no directors, no public, and no press. You know that I have a good nose."

The judgment was unequivocal. The Russian theater was not prepared to recognize what this man was asking of it.

The Russian theater was mired in a state of corruption, out of which the Moscow Art Theater was to rise and lead a way. Unfortunately neither was it going to be able to realize and project the personal quality of Chekhov. But it was to present the author with something to which he no longer attached much value: success. Chekhov now no longer felt that he was responsible for the stage flop of *The Sea Gull*. Only a few weeks after the disappointment in Saint Petersburg, despite his vow, he finished *Uncle Vanya*, the new version of *The Wood Demon*. Yet he did not consider giving the play to a theater.

Nemirovich-Danchenko, a much-performed dramatist and the partner of Stanislavsky, was one of Chekhov's friends. At the time, he was the director of a school of drama in Moscow. This school, which included Meyerhold among its talented students, merged with Stanislavsky's Society for Literature and Art, and the two men founded the Moscow Art Theater. The name tells what the founders wanted to achieve: a theater dedicated to art. Of course, they did not mean that "high art," which was the goal of the court theaters—but true art: the art of truth. It was also to be a theater devoted to realism and naturalism—according to Zola's concepts. It was Nemirovich-Danchenko who discovered the author

Chekhov and brought him to this theater. Stanislav-sky was by no means certain of Chekhov's merit and had to be convinced.

Chekhov, however, was not at all the dramatist the new directors believed they had discovered and were now preparing to put on the stage. He, like most European dramatists at the time, had already gone beyond the stage of realism. But the new spirit of his drama was understood by only a few, who, like Gorky, Meyerhold, Kommissarzhevskaya, belonged to the younger generation. This should be made clear before we go on to speak of the triumph of *The Sea Gull* on December 17, 1898, in its premiere at the Moscow Art Theater.

The preliminary events were interesting. Nemiro-vich-Danchenko pressed Chekhov to reconsider the matter of allowing another production of the play, because the new theater urgently needed the work of a modern Russian dramatist for its first season. Nemirovich-Danchenko kept on writing and begging for the play until Chekhov finally stopped answering his letters. Now the new directors decided to present the dramatist with a *fait accompli*. By the end of August, when Chekhov heard about it, the company had been rehearsing for weeks.

At once, Chekhov traveled to Moscow. He at-tended the rehearsals of Count Alexey Tolstoy's his-torical play *Czar Fyodor*, which was to be presented at the theater's inauguration, a play in the Meininger manner and under Stanislavsky's direction. It im-pressed Chekhov greatly—probably because the role of the Czarina was played by Olga Knipper, the enchanting and temperamental actress, whom he was to love and marry.

After Chekhov saw two rehearsals without cos-tumes and makeup, he had to leave Moscow—"for he had to settle an affair he could not postpone—with his bacteria." The last conversations with Stanislavsky were unpleasant. Chekhov did not like him. In Chekhov's eyes, Stanislavsky's acting of Trigorin and the whiny performance of the actress who played Nina were insufferable. From Yalta, where his health improved somewhat, he wrote polite letters, and he sent a congratulatory note on the opening-night success of *Czar Fyodor*.

No doubt, he was perfectly sincere when he wrote to Nemirovich-Danchenko that the new theater was to begin a new page of fame in the history of the Russian stage. He recognized that here the art of acting was taken very seriously and was being raised above the present state of corruption and mediocrity. He recognized that the new path his associates were taking was the only one through which the new goals could be achieved. The goals, however, were not his own, and the direction was not one that would lead to his plays being presented as he conceived them.

In his memoirs, Stanislavsky described the premiere of *The Sea Gull*. It so influenced the future of his new theater that the sea gull was chosen for its emblem, which it is to this day. "When the first act ended, there was dead silence in the auditorium. One of the actresses fainted, and I myself felt such despair that I could hardly manage to stand on my legs. Then, suddenly, after a long pause, the audience broke into wild noise, shouts of bravo, and thunderous applause." And that is how it went. "We felt as if it was Easter Eve. Telegrams went to Yalta, and Chekhov answered, 'Tell everyone that I am unspeakably grateful. I feel chained to Yalta like Dreyfus is to Devil's Island. I am sorry not to be with you. The telegrams have made me happy.'"

But his evaluation did not change. He did not attend one performance in Moscow, even when he had recuperated. In February 1899 the two directors came to visit him, to wrest from him the permission to do *Uncle Vanya*, which, in the meantime, he had promised the Imperial Maly Theater. "I don't know your theater," he said. "I must see first how you present plays." At the end of April, when the theater was already closed, Chekhov visited his sister in Moscow. Nemirovich-Danchenko and Stanislavsky had an almost mad idea. As their own theater was in the process of being rebuilt, they rented another, in which to give Chekhov a private performance of *The Sea Gull*. The actors performed without makeup and costumes, in their street-clothes, and on an empty stage.

It came to an altercation that tells more about the true Chekhov than do the prettied-up reports of the unhappy directors. After the third act, during intermission, he appeared on the stage, explaining that it was not necessary to perform the last act—the three acts that had been played were not his own. And he demanded that the role of Nina be recast at once. When it was explained to him that it was impossible, he screamed that he would forbid any further performances. Olga Knipper, who trembled as she witnessed this scene, said later that it seemed impossible to her that a man who was usually so polite was capable of such brutality.

A few days later, Chekhov wrote to Gorky that Stanislavsky's acting had been like that of a "paralytic." Yet he admitted: "As a whole, it was somewhat absorbing. Only at some points, I could not believe that I had written this play." But, what was more important was that he now realized that the Art Theater was better than the Maly. He gave his consent when Stanislavsky succeeded in getting the Maly to relinquish *Uncle Vanya* to the Art Theater. He also promised to come to rehearsals.

But he did not appear. On October 1, when rehearsals began, he sent a telegram with good wishes, which showed that he had come to feel some warmth toward the ensemble. He even consented to being photographed with the ensemble during a reading. It was a posed picture—the reading really never took place. The premiere of *Uncle Vanya*, which Chekhov did not attend, was only a moderate success. Chekhov consoled the actors: "I have been writing for twenty-one years and know that a moderate success is the best thing for an author and for the actors."

Nemirovich-Danchenko and Stanislavsky begged him to write a play expressly for the Art Theater. He hesitated for a long time. But he looked forward to stimulation and pleasure if the ensemble were to tour in the Crimea. He also knew, of course, that Olga, to whom he had declared his love, would be with them. Now the ailing Chekhov was to experience the happiest, gayest times of these last years— he was host to a whole theatrical company. Olga arrived eight days before the others, and Chekhov and Olga traveled together to Sevastopol, where the tour was to begin. There, pale and tired, Chekhov sat through the performance of *Uncle Vanya*. It is said that he bravely tried to smile. He went home before *The Sea Gull* was to be performed, explaining that he had already seen it. The company took the boat to Yalta, where it gave eleven performances. In Yalta, everyone spent their free time in Chekhov's house. It was one big party. And now a kind of reconciliation with Stanislavsky seems to have occurred, and Stanislavsky reported that from then on their relationship was more cordial. As he always did,

Chekhov now enjoyed the company of actors and the atmosphere of gaiety.

During the weeks when Chekhov was working on *The Three Sisters*, Olga wrote imploring letters from Moscow, asking him to marry her. "You do have a beating heart, why do you pretend to be so unfeeling?" But Chekhov, who knew how close to death he was, did not want to tie the young woman to himself. Constantly his work on the new play was interrupted by illness. Stanislavsky came to see him: the theatrical season was about to begin. With great effort Chekhov forced himself to finish the play. He himself brought the manuscript to Moscow. After he heard the first reading he was convinced that no one understood what he wanted to say. There was another furious scene with Stanislavsky. After that, he journeyed home. Nemirovich-Danchenko tried to mediate, but Chekhov would not budge. He wrote to Olga that the play was bound to fail, and that he would never again write for the Moscow Art Theater. He did not attend the premiere, which took place on January 31, 1901. It was not a success. There were only a few curtain calls. Chekhov wrote: "One can write for the theater in Germany, in Sweden, even in Italy, but not in Russia where people have no respect for a playwright and will kick him if he doesn't watch out."

Five months later, in the summer of 1901, in a small Moscow church, very quietly, Chekhov married Olga. He called her his "little German," because her father was an Alsatian. On their honeymoon, on the way to a sanatorium near Ufa, they visited Gorky, who was under house arrest in Nizhni Novgorod. The couple was usually happy when they were together. And every separation tormented each of them, though in different ways. They wrote daily letters or telegrams to each other. Chekhov wrote that he envied the rat under the floor of the theater where she was performing. He once signed himself "your aged archmonk." When Olga found that she was pregnant, she became hysterical. She wrote tormenting letters, which Chekhov answered wearily. After she miscarried, she became seriously ill. When she was brought home to Yalta, she had to be carried off the steamboat into the house. The doctors would not permit Chekhov to stay with her.

The second event that marked Chekhov's last years had happened in 1897, several months after the disappointing opening night of *The Sea Gull*. It was his death sentence. While he was dining with Suvorin, who was visiting him in Moscow, at the Hermitage restaurant, he had a hemorrhage. Blood gushed from his mouth. He asked for ice to stop the bleeding, but it continued. He was brought to Suvorin's hotel room, and a doctor was called. Two days later, the attacks had become so severe that he had to be brought to a hospital. It was the first time that he let himself be treated by colleagues. They ordered him to change his way of life, give up his practice and all his community work. But the latter he never gave up. Tolstoy visited the patient in the hospital. He spoke, tactfully, of immortality. But Chekhov responded, "I have no need of it."

Chekhov spent the fall and winter of 1897 and 1898 in Biarritz and Nice. Then the decision was made that he give up the estate in Melikhovo and build a house in Yalta. Land next to a Cossack cemetery was purchased. ("Above all," Suvorin remarked, "he loved circuses and cemeteries.") The building of the house and the planning of the garden gave him great pleasure. There was a view, through cypresses, of the sea. But soon he began to hate his "warm

Siberia"—especially during Olga's absences. He suffered boredom from the idleness that the frequent attacks now forced upon him: "Every day I catch two mice, so that no one can say I'm doing nothing."

The physical act of writing became increasingly difficult. In February 1903 he began to write *The Cherry Orchard*. "I write five lines a day, and even that causes me unbearable pain."

Tikhonov wrote the following about a night he spent with Chekhov in June 1902.

> I did not want to leave Chekhov alone in the empty house; so I slept in the room next to his own. I was worried about him. Through the thin wall I could hear him coughing. I had never known him to have such long and severe coughing spells I heard him get out of bed several times, pace up and down in the room, drink something from a glass, lie down, start to cough again, and again jump out of bed. Finally I fell asleep. I woke in the middle of the night, with an oppressive sense of impending danger. . . . Thunder and lightning were shaking the house, and suddenly I seemed to hear beyond the roar of the thunderstorm a long, drawn-out groan. I pressed my ear against the wall behind which Chekhov was lying. My suspicion was confirmed; again I heard that tortured, almost inhuman groan, now interrupted by vomiting —or sobbing. I believed Chekhov lay dying. Beside myself with fear, I ran, in my nightshirt and barefoot, through the dining room, into his bedroom. . . .
>
> The thunderstorm, as it often happens, had reached a climax and now subsided for a few moments. Suddenly the house seemed still and

sinister. Again, in the silence, I heard suppressed groaning, coughing, and a gurgling sound. I pushed the door open and whispered, "Anton Pavlovich?"

Next to the bed, on a low stool, stood an almost burned-out candle. Chekhov lay on his side, in a jumble of sheets. He trembled, jerking convulsively, and his long neck with its prominent Adam's apple was bent over the edge of the bed. The coughing spell shook his whole body, and with each jerk blood streamed from his wide-open mouth into a blue enameled spittoon.

The thunderstorm was raging again, though Chekhov did not notice it. Again I called out his name. He moved his head back onto the pillows. He wiped the blood from his beard and mustache and searched me out slowly with his eyes.

There, in the yellow light of the flickering candle, I saw his eyes for the first time without their usual pince-nez: large eyes, helpless like those of a child. Their whites had yellowed because of the great physical exertion. Chekhov spoke softly, and with great difficulty: "I have disturbed your sleep . . . forgive me . . . my friend."

Now the doctors who treated him declared that the Crimea really did not agree with him. They advised him to spend the summer in the country near Moscow. Stanislavsky gave the Chekhovs the use of his *dacha*. But Chekhov could not bear staying there. In July 1903, despite all, they traveled back to Yalta.

In September, when rehearsals for *The Cherry Orchard* were about to begin, Olga arrived in Moscow—without the play. Finally, on October 12, Chekhov wrote that the *comedy* was finished. Nemirovich-

Danchenko and Stanislavsky answered that this was no comedy but a "tragedy of Russian life." Chekhov shook his head: what could he say? "They will make it into another tear-jerker."

In December he went to Moscow. *The Cherry Orchard* was to open on January 17, 1904. The directors decided to celebrate on that day Chekhov's birthday and an anniversary of Chekhov's years as a writer. It was to be one of the grand events of the Moscow season. Chekhov protested—not only because this was not the right date—but was not heeded. The directors were relentless; they were going to have their theater event. Everything was prepared, including a tribute that was to be paid to Chekhov onstage, with speeches and a presentation of gifts. (When Stanislavsky asked Chekhov what he would like to receive, the answer was, an enema syringe.) There was great horror that evening: Chekhov did not appear. Shortly before the end of the third act, he finally arrived. The actor Vishnevsky, the old friend and companion of his youth in Taganrog, almost had to use force to get him to come. When he came on the stage, the audience gave him a great ovation. There he stood, hardly able to suppress his coughing as he had to listen to the endless speeches. Seeing the deathly ill author, standing bent over, trying to force an artificial smile while patiently suffering pain, moved some of the people in the orchestra seats to call for a chair. But he waved it away.

The play was not a great success. Two days after the premiere Chekhov wrote to an acquaintance: "At the premiere of my play I was honored, and so amply that I still haven't recovered from it."

At Yalta, where the stream of visitors never came to a stop, he was forced to take opium in order to bear the pain. It was at that time that he wrote to

Olga the passage quoted earlier: "You ask me, 'what is life?' You might as well have asked 'what is a carrot?' A carrot is a carrot, and one knows no more about it."

When the doctors advised him to go to Badenweiler, in the Black Forest in Germany, he said to Ivan Bunin (the great storyteller and later Nobel prize winner): "I am going away to die like a dog." He traveled with Olga, stopping in Berlin to consult a specialist. At first, the treatment seemed to give him some relief. But soon his condition grew worse. The owner of the villa the Chekhovs had rented asked that they move out. In his last days one could see him sit on his balcony in the Hotel Sommer. To the very end he did not lose his sense of humor. This is proved by Olga's account of the improvised story he told to amuse her on the night he lay dying.

When his breathing became more laborious, Olga sent for their doctor. He had oxygen brought to Chekhov, and ordered that he drink some champagne. Quietly, Chekhov asked him, in German, "*Tod?*" Chekhov's last words, too, were in German: "*Ich sterbe.*"

In a zinc casket, the body of Chekhov made the long journey to Russia. When the casket arrived in Moscow, on a hot and humid day, on July 9, 1904, Gorky and Chaliapin came to the railway station to meet their dead friend. On another platform, a military band struck up a march: a dead general was being honored. The freight car, which had brought Chekhov's body, was marked with a sign "Fresh Oysters."

The speeches and deportment of the hundred people who attended the funeral was of a kind that the weeping Chaliapin cursed, "And for these miserable people he lived and worked!"

4.

This short biography would not be complete without the following little epilogue.

Chekhov did not possess, as I have said, a *Weltanschauung*. He was not religious and had no faith in ideologies. But in his last years, his judgments and his convictions were of a clarity that knew no compromise. Tolstoy said of him that he was "truly a good man." Goodness in Chekhov was truthfulness and justice.

His view was that writers and artists should not meddle in politics—unless politics meddle and interfere with artistic work. "There are enough public prosecutors, district attorneys, and policemen." But this opinion did not prevent him from making decisions and expressing views that reveal him as an intransigent enemy of the system under which he had to live. Gorky reported that Chekhov said—in 1901, after the suppression of the student rebellion—that there were going to be clashing confrontations in Russia; first yearly, then monthly, and within ten or fifteen years, it would come to a point where the country would be ripe for a constitution. In this sense he believed in progress:

> So far, it is just the students, the young men and young women at the universities; they are honest and decent people—our hope and Russia's future. But when they grow up, our hopes are transformed and Russia's future goes up in smoke. All that remains in the filter is doctors, owners of villas, undernourished civil servants, and corrupt engineers. . . . I have no belief in our intelligentsia. It is hypocritical, false, hysterical,

and lazy. I don't even believe in it when it suffers and laments, because its oppressors come right out of its own midst. I believe, rather, in individual human beings who are scattered throughout the country, be they peasants or intellectuals; in them lies our strength, even if there are only a few of them . . . for one can see their work. However that may be, science progresses, social consciousness is growing, and we are beginning to be troubled by questions of morality. . . .

Chekhov the physician had a knowledge of human beings. He knew mankind too well to believe in sweeping change. "It is said that in the end truth will conquer. That is not true. . . . For each intelligent human being there are a thousand numskulls." He had no liking for the Marxists and spoke of "their pompous attitudes." He did not put much stock in Marxism.

When our socialists exploit a cholera epidemic to serve their goals, I begin to despise them. When despicable means are used to serve excellent goals, they make these goals hateful. . . . If I were a politician, I would never be able to make the decision to dishonor the present in order to serve the future—even if one was to promise me for one gram of infamous lies a hundred kilograms of future happiness.

In Chekhov's lifetime, no one knew that the Czar had bestowed upon him a title of nobility for the service he had rendered in improving the school system. He would have been ashamed to mention an honor received by a system he loathed. During the Dreyfus affair he broke publicly with Suvorin, his best friend, because Suvorin's press fell upon the innocent man "like a pack of hungry jackals." In 1902 Chekhov publicly withdrew from the Imperial Academy (which he had been nominated to in 1900) when, upon the order of Czar Nicholas II, the nomination of Gorky was vetoed.

When the twenty-two-year-old Lenin read Chekhov's long story *Ward Number 6*, he felt "real anxiety. . . . I could not stay any longer in my room, and got up and went out. I had the feeling that I myself was locked in at *Ward Number 6*."

Lenin described exactly the impression Chekhov wanted to elicit in his readers and audience.

CHEKHOV AND
THE CRAFT OF THE THEATER

In 1902, Chekhov wrote to Alexander Tikhonov:

> You say you wept over my plays. You are not the only one. But I did not write them for this. It was Stanislavsky who made them so tearful. I intended something quite different.

Chekhov's judgment of Stanislavsky's productions of the Chekhov plays—as numerous passages from letters and witnesses' observations testify—can be summarized in a sentence he wrote about the production of *The Cherry Orchard* a few weeks before his death: "Stanislavsky has ruined my play."

It is said that dramatists cannot judge the productions of their plays. That may be true of those who do not understand the theater, but not of Chekhov, who knew and understood the stage. When he was still an adolescent in Taganrog his favorite pastime was attending the theater. When he went to Moscow as a nineteen-year-old, to study medicine and to rescue his family from their poverty-stricken life, the theater attracted him more than anything else. He wrote his stories to earn a living. Now that a heavily edited draft of "Play without a Title" (*Platonov*)—on which he must have worked for a long time and with much passion—has been found among his posthumous papers, we know what really was in his thoughts.

When Chekhov was writing this play, he had a plan, a program for the theater. Later, for a while, he abandoned this plan and made concessions to the conventional stage. But in his major works he returned to his Platonov plan. His contemporaries found the newness and innovation of this plan so strange and shocking that they hooted two Chekhov plays off the stage on opening nights. Not one of his plays was a success in its first production. His works needed time to succeed. The reason was not, as their later success has proved, a lack of dramatic effectiveness, but rather their unusualness. There were times when Chekhov went daily to the theater, to study the conditions of the stage and the conduct and attitudes of the actors. One of these periods occurred while *The Sea Gull* was in rehearsal. His understanding of actors was extremely astute. After all, he eventually was to be married to an actress. One of his contemporaries who worked in the theater reported: "Every false note, every cliché, every fatuous or vulgar nuance made Chekhov wince. . . . Often he would interrupt the actors and plead, 'Please, no theatricality! Let it be simple, just simple!' "

So far, Chekhov's judgment of Stanislavsky's Chekhov theater has not been taken seriously. The Chekhov tradition as originally conceived by the Moscow Art Theater became dated not because there was a quest for the kind of theater Chekhov really had in mind, but rather because of the great changes in theater in general throughout the world. Surprisingly, some of the Chekhov productions in recent years are closer to the concepts of the true Chekhov theater than is the conventional style for producing Chekhov, whose alleged authenticity originated with Stanislavsky. I have in mind: the Milan production of *Platonov*, directed by Giorgio Strehler; the Stockholm production of *The Sea Gull*, directed by Ingmar Bergman; *The Three Sisters*, produced in Stuttgart under the direction of Rudolf Noelte and, also produced in Stuttgart, *The Cherry Orchard*, directed by Peter Zadek; and the Prague production of *The Three Sisters*, under the direction of Otomar Krejča. I shall return to these productions in my chapter on European stage productions.

While Chekhov was still alive, the true plan and character of Chekhov's work was recognized by some of the younger people. Among those who early appreciated the true Chekhov was Vera Kommissarzhevskaya. She was Chekhov's favorite among the actresses who worked in his plays. (She was the first Sea Gull in the unfortunate Saint Petersburg production that was booed off the stage.) She was among the young rebels who broke early with Stanislavsky. Chekhov wanted to write a play for her after she had left Stanislavsky's ensemble. In her own theater, which she and her brother directed, she provided Meyerhold with a chance for his revolutionary experiments. Meyerhold, another of the young rebels, also had been an actor of the Art Theater and a student of Stanislavsky. He had portrayed Treplev in the famous *Sea Gull* production of 1898. Meyerhold discovered in Chekhov's dramaturgy "new paths that are closed to the methods of psychological realism." He sharply criticized Stanislavsky's overuse of the scenic details that he loved so (an "ocean of objects"), and the

sentimental atmosphere, which had made Stanislavsky's production of *The Cherry Orchard* so intoler-
able to Chekhov. For the third act, in which a ball is
taking place while the news about the sale of the
cherry orchard is expected, Meyerhold demanded a
cold and hard delivery, the projection of a "nightmare," a "horror"; he wrote to Chekhov, "Your play is
abstract like a symphony." When Meyerhold in the
style of that period spoke of "symbolism" or even
"mysticism," he meant to characterize the antirealistic
element in Chekhov's plays, the "rhythmic movement" of the work as a whole.

Especially revealing are the observations of Gorky,
whom Chekhov loved as a human being, whose
talent he recognized at once, and whom he reprimanded for his carelessness as an artist (he has no
sense of architecture, doesn't know how to build). "Do
you know what you are doing?" Gorky wrote to
Chekhov in 1900. "You are flogging realism to death!
And it will soon be dead for a long time." Gorky
sensed the fundamental tension between the musical-
ity and the coldness in these plays and recognized,
above all, their great art of simplicity: "You are a man
who can create a character with a mere word, and
with a sentence tell a story." This brings to mind
Chekhov's words: "The most important thing is to
construct a sentence." Gorky said of *Uncle Vanya*
that he saw more meaning in this play than others
did, something "powerful," which he too called "symbolism." Chekhov, in turn, wrote that Gorky deserved
great merit for being the first writer in Russia and in
the whole world to express contempt and revulsion
for the *meshchanstvo* (usually translated as "petty
bourgeoisie," or as "that conservative stratum of society that stagnates in personal egotism," or as "the
establishment") and so stimulated the protest of

others. Chekhov shared in this protest, but he wanted to do more—he wanted to provoke this protest in the audience. After writing the lines to Tikhonov, quoted at the beginning of this chapter, Chekhov continued:

> I wanted to say simply and honestly, "Look at yourselves, look how badly and boringly you lead your lives!" The most important thing is that people come to recognize this. As soon as they understand it, they will have to live differently and better. I will not live to see it, but I am convinced that life will be quite different then, not to be compared with that of today. But in the meantime I will not stop from repeatedly saying to people: "Just look how boringly and badly you are living!" Yet what is there to weep about?

Chekhov's is "a theater that shows, that exposes," to quote from Ilya Ehrenburg's essay, in which he pleaded that the modern and contemporary quality in Chekhov be recognized.

Gorky expressed it thus:

> Chekhov understood, with a high measure of art, how to recognize and describe the trivial in life. . . . The trivial always found in him a severe critic. . . . This great, wise man, who observed everything, who encountered this boring, gray mass of weak people, looked at the lazy inhabitants of his homeland and said to them, with a sad smile and in a tone of mild but profound reproach, with an expression of hopeless sorrow,— "Ladies and gentlemen, you are living badly!"

Vakhtangov, another revolutionary of the Russian theater, who directed Gerhart Hauptmann's *Friedens-*

fest ("the Feast of Reconciliation") in the Studio, was reprimanded by Stanislavsky's partner Nemirovich-Danchenko because he brought out the "shrill tones" too sharply. Gorky stood by the young director. Gorky severely opposed the "mania to muffle and mute everything," which had angered him previously in Stanislavsky's production of *The Lower Depths.* He demanded instead, in the sense of Chekhov, "genuine art"—the art of protest.

But we must beware of being unjust. Stanislavsky's historical merit cannot be ignored. It will not be diminished by the observation that he led the Russian theater in a direction different from the one Chekhov had in mind. Perhaps even, considering the course of history, his was the only direction possible. Chekhov's goals were perhaps too much in advance of the times to be comprehensible to his contemporaries. His aggressive opposition to the theater as he found it was as clear as that of Stanislavsky. It was the aggressive opposition of their generation—that of the youth of that epoch in Europe. In 1881, when Chekhov was in the process of finishing his work on *Platonov,* Zola wrote, urging that naturalism be utilized for the stage. He expressed what moved them all: anger toward the pompousness, the dishonesty, the corruption of the theater, a theater that was dominated by the pathos with which the tragedies were presented and the overacting of the stars. The new password was: reality and truth. But years were to pass before reality and truth would reach the Russian stage: in 1887 it would reach the Théâtre Libre in Paris (Antoine); in 1889, the Freie Bühne in Berlin (Otto Brahm, Hauptmann); in 1892, the Independent Theatre in London (Grein, Shaw); in 1896, the Moscow Art Theater. Reading Stanislavsky's memoirs, one gains some insight into the many difficulties and obstacles he had to overcome, from the day he founded the Moscow Society for Art and Literature (in 1888), whose niveau Chekhov hardly took seriously, until he could finally back up his opposition to the present state of the theater with a viable program for the future. Perhaps he would not have been able to achieve this had he not met Nemirovich-Danchenko, his intellectual and literary collaborator. Taking all this into account, one has to admire even more the genius of Chekhov. The *Platonov* play of the twenty-one-year-old Chekhov was written before the publication of Zola's pamphlet, and at a time when Stanislavsky was still dreaming of nothing but operettas and vaudevilles.

The Russian theater, of course, had an advantage over that of the rest of Europe. Since Gogol and Stchepkin, and the first production of Gogol's *Government Inspector* in 1836, it had a tradition of realism. This satirical comedy was even part of the repertoire of the Imperial Theater. It is indeed astonishing that its performance was tolerated in this land where despotism ruthlessly suppressed the slightest expression of an independent impulse. But the Czar was amused when he saw civil servants satirized. The aristocracy, more and more hard-pressed by the rising bourgeoisie, encouraged derision of the new capitalist class. And so Ostrovsky could become the program director of the Imperial Theater. It was in the year of Ostrovsky's death that Tolstoy wrote the naturalistic peasant drama *The Power of Darkness*. However, it was not to be performed until 1889, and then in Paris, by Antoine, not in Russia.

The form of satire seduced the Russian dramatists and actors into caricature. But in Chekhov's plan there was no place for caricature. "Even if it were in the interest of the theater to caricature human beings, it would be a lie. It is simply unnecessary. A caricature, of course, will sharpen an image and so be more easily understood. But it is better to work out the drawing of a sketch with care than to smear it up with showy and shoddy strokes."

Caricaturing actors have a tendency to hamming. In their indignation at the low niveau of the Russian theater Stanislavsky and Chekhov were in agreement. The actors were despised by society and often led slovenly, debauched lives. Many of them became alcoholics. Only those who were able to rise to a position in the Imperial Theaters were guaranteed a measure of respectability. But even there conditions were in an unbelievable state of muddle and slovenliness. Chekhov believed, as I mentioned earlier, that the major cause of the scandalous uproar and failure of the 1887 premiere of *Ivanov* was that the actors did not know their lines and that they were drunk by the last act. He reported that what had been recited on the stage was unbelievable. In 1882 this was his judgment: "The Russian actor has everything—except education, culture, and manners, in the good sense of the word." Besides the slovenly bungling, he found the stars' method of upstaging the rest of the cast, the acting up front before the footlights, especially distasteful. And exactly this, despite all his admiration, he had already criticized in 1881 in the acting style of Sarah Bernhardt, who was the rage of the Moscow audience when she played there on tour: "She wants to be striking, to amaze." It was the style of the *coup de théâtre*, the objective of which was to exhibit the virtuosity of the stars. The *coup de théâtre* was the style of *La Tosca* and *La Dame aux Camélias* and other plays by Sardou and Dumas fils. These writers had given up romantic melodrama and were devoting themselves to what was considered realistic theater at the time. But what they deemed "dramatic" was identical with effect. The material was taken "from life," not because it was life that was to be shown, but because this material yielded effects with which a Bernhardt could bring an audience to their knees. The same exaggeration that blurred and hammed up what was truly comic also blurred and hammed up the tragic. With the one it became caricature; with the other it resulted in *coup de théâtre*.

One can imagine what a great impression the Meininger troupe, during their 1885 tour, made on the young Russians, who had read Zola and wished to see resurrected on the Russian stage what once Pushkin, Gogol, and Turgenev had realized—and what Tolstoy and Dostoyevsky now were achieving in the novel (1877, *Anna Karenina*; 1880, *The Brothers Karamazov*; 1886, *The Death of Ivan Ilyich*). In the troupe's performances seriousness, accuracy, and discipline worked in ensemble: it was a "holiday of art," as Stanislavsky wrote. Their productions, with their spirit of solidity and seriousness, made a lasting impression on the young Russians interested in drama. Yet people, even Stanislavsky, also took exception to the exaggeratedly emotional acting of the Germans.

These two principles—solidity and seriousness—were to form the cornerstone of the Moscow Art Theater. And Chekhov understood well what an advance these new standards would bring about in the Russian theater. To have them succeed was a historical feat and accomplishment, and Chekhov did not withhold recognition of this achievement. He never did like Stanislavsky, though he later respected him, but he felt warm sympathy for Nemirovich-Danchenko. He felt even more warmth for the actors, whose esprit de corps and sense of ensemble-playing he praised. He would have felt much warmth toward them even if he had not found his future wife, Olga Knipper, among them. What these actors did on the stage for the sake of art and truth moved him deeply. "One must wrest the stage out of the hands of the merchants," he said, "and give it over into the hands of literary people; otherwise it will perish." Yet it was clear to him, from the time of the production of *The Sea Gull* in 1898 to that of *The Cherry Orchard* in 1904, that the director and the actors of the Art Theater took the path to his plays "without me." They believed they knew better than he did. And their success seemed to prove them right. Stanislavsky—who always thought of himself as "a slow one"—deserves respect for describing the late insight he gained while writing his memoirs in 1925—an insight that, as he wrote, gave him "new horizons":

> The works of all geniuses who, like Chekhov, represent a cornerstone, outlive generations; generations do not outlive them. . . . It is possible that some of what is Chekhov, in this or that work, may appear dated and for the postrevolutionary era no longer valid—yet Chekhov, in *how* he has presented his material, has not even begun to come to full flower in our theater. The chapter about Chekhov in the history of our theater is far from finished; we have not yet studied him thoroughly enough, have not yet penetrated to his inner essence. We have closed the book prematurely. We must open it anew, to study it thoroughly and read to the end.

Stanislavsky had not understood the *how* in Chekhov. He had distorted the *how* because of his fixation on elements that, though contained in Chekhov's work, he had interpreted wrongly. He directed theater of atmosphere—mood theater—and the mood, which dominated this theater, was that of ennui. In Chekhov, mood is an element among others, though one he knew how to use as few have before him. And ennui was for him the opposite of what Stanislavsky made of it. That is, it was not to Chekhov tearful, melancholic, elegiac, sentimental. It was something hateful, as it would be for a man who suffered bitterly from ennui after he was forced (by his physicians) to endure it—a man who, according to Gorky, conceived of work as the basis of all culture and civilization. What Chekhov brought to the stage as boredom or "ennui" is best translated as "emptiness." This ennui, this boredom of his epoch, is only superficially different from that of today: we, of course, have the added element of noise.

The consciousness of emptiness, then as today, is numbing. And it is as hateful today as it was then because those who suffer it have no desire and no courage to face the truth, as it is, and to draw from that the necessary conclusions. It is this which Kierkegaard calls "indifference"—and nothing enraged Chekhov more, as we know, than to be accused of "indifference": "I hate lies and violence in any form. . . . Don't I protest, from the beginning to the end, against the lie?" This hateful thing has to be protested, as Gorky had demanded and Vakhtangov had done. The worst one can do with it is to transform it into mood. To lull the audience into a sniveling, tearful sentimentality relieves it of the task which Chekhov meant to confront it with. As he so often said,

> They [the audience] shall be the jury: they have to reach the verdict. The artist's task is to observe, to choose, to unmask, to sum up. And these tasks presuppose a question. If there is no

question asked to begin with, there is nothing to unmask, to expose, to select. . . . Those are right who demand that the artist must have a conscious relationship to his work. But they often confuse two concepts: the solution of the question, and the right way of asking it. The commitment of the artist is only to the second task. . . . It is the duty of the court to formulate the problem correctly, but it is up to the members of the jury to solve it, each according to his own insight.

Chekhov once observed that it would seem very agreeable to combine art and sermon, and then to put the whole burden on "the gospel" that is being preached, without first bringing the reader or the audience to the point where they can believe in that gospel. For him, he said, this would be simply "technically impossible." He said, "When I present a horse thief, they want me to say, it is bad to steal a horse. But everyone knows that well enough, without my saying so."

Chekhov's basic principle is scientific: it is objectivity. Its application demands extreme coolness. "Only he who is cool is just." True justice determines the organization of the material, which has to be presented both objectively and convincingly, if "the jurors" are to discover the truth. In this, above all, the controversy with Stanislavsky came to a head. For Stanislavsky believed that it was the task of the director to reinforce the mood, to make it as inescapable as possible, through details and stage effects.

Meyerhold reported that in the scene in *The Sea Gull* in which Arkadina says farewell to the servants, Chekhov had specified that there be three of them. Stanislavsky, however, had a whole mass of people come onto the stage, among whom was a woman with a crying baby in her arms. "Why this?" Chekhov asked him. The answer was, that this was "just like in real life" and "realistic." Chekhov laughed, "So, this is realistic!" After a brief silence he continued: "But this is the stage—and the stage is art! If you take a good portrait painting, cut out the nose, and put into the hole a real nose, that is realistic—but the painting is ruined."

As for the crying baby Chekhov said, "This is superfluous. It is as if you play pianissimo on the piano and the lid falls, crashing down on the keys." Again, the answer was that it was often like this in real life, and that often a forte, suddenly, breaks into a pianissimo.

"Undoubtedly," Chekhov replied. "But the stage has its own conditions. Don't you know that you don't have a fourth wall? The theater is art; it expresses the quintessence of life. It is unnecessary to fill it up with superfluous details."

The quintessence is contained in the text. What is not in the text must not be brought onto the stage. He was cross when the actors begged him to explain their parts to them. "It is all written down in the text. I am just a doctor." It was indeed all written down in the text.

This is how Chekhov described one part of his *Platonov* plan:

> In real life people don't spend every minute shooting each other, hanging themselves, or making declarations of love. They don't dedicate their time to saying intelligent things. They spend much more of it eating, drinking, flirting, and saying foolish things—and that is what should happen on the stage. Someone should

write a play in which people come and go, eat, talk about the weather, and play cards. Life should be exactly as it is, and people should be exactly as complicated and at the same time exactly as simple as they are in life. People eat a meal, and at the same time their happiness is made or their lives are being ruined.

That has sounds of Zola. But what is decisive is not the goal, not the imitation of reality, but the method. It is the opposite of the "well-made play," the *pièce-bien-faite*, as, from Eugène Scribe (1791-1861) to Henrik Ibsen (1828-1906), it has been "dramatically" developed.

Chekhov was not fond of Ibsen: "He doesn't understand anything about life." Ibsen himself admitted that he had learned his dramatic technique from that of the well-made play. According to its pattern, he had constructed his plot, which, by means of its dramatic climax, proved its effectiveness as theater. Chekhov believed that plot is unimportant for the stage. He rejected "the dramatic" when it was the result of calculated effect. His friends in the theater rebuked him because, allegedly, he did not understand "dramatic" as they understood it. Six years after writing *Platonov* he was ready to make a compromise —in *Ivanov*. It failed—because the gap between the truth he sought to show and the stage effects he was utilizing could not be bridged.

The method Chekhov discovered as he designed the *Platonov* plan (more correctly, he *re*discovered it, for the Greeks and Shakespeare had known this plan before him) was that of the dual planes of the stage—one of which is indirect. When people talk to one another, the truth usually is not contained in what they say but rather in what they do not say.

They talk in order to talk. They talk, often without answering each other. They talk past each other, each preoccupied with himself. They talk, in order to deceive themselves. There is always a pause, because they either don't understand one another or they don't really hear one another. But in these pauses life goes on; decisive things can happen in these intervals of silence. And so Chekhov discovered (rediscovered) the dramatic meaning of silence.

This was both understood and misunderstood in the Moscow Art Theater. Indeed, Nemirovich-Danchenko and Stanislavsky recognized the uniqueness in Chekhov's indirect method. Chekhov's method was to bring about a revolution in the art of the theater and was even to shed new light on the presentation of the works of a Sophocles or a Shakespeare. A contemporary of Chekhov's described the technique that evolved from this indirect method:

> The inner dialogue, and the charm of that which is only half-expressed—this was what the performers of the Art Theater projected. Chekhov had abolished the old concept of plot and action, and now the theater discovered that the word is far from being the most important element in the art of the theater. The word is only an indication of inner emotions, one that is neither complete nor perfect but only a guide that can lead to the soul of the character. But often and at the most dramatic moments the word becomes mute and yields to silence. This silence is full of meaning, full of the whole energy of the spoken words that have gone before, and of the latent presence of the thousands of words that are to follow or that perhaps will never be said. This silence is stronger than the

most violent scream, and it contains more meaning than a hundred words that are determined by a defined meaning. Thus the goal of the drama becomes his silence. And it must be acted out and projected so that it resounds and breaks out into a thousand colors.

The Moscow Art Theater staged Chekhov's silence in exaggerated ways. First, they padded it with innumerable details of silent acting, with such effects as the crying baby in the farewell scene in *The Cherry Orchard*, in their effort to achieve the "purest" reality. Second, they strove with all their resources to express emotions through silent acting, so that the audience simply could not overlook what went on in the "inner dialogue." Chekhov felt that this was not his but another kind of theater, and exactly the theater he wanted to avoid. Here is an example.

In the last scene of *Uncle Vanya* there occurs, again, a leave-taking. Astrov, the doctor, a central character, steps up to a map of Africa that hangs on the wall and says, "The heat must be awful in Africa now just awful!" Olga Knipper wrote to her future husband how marvelously Stanislavsky played this scene: "How much bitterness, how much experience of life he expressed in that line! And how he pronounced the words, with a kind of bravura that was most exciting!" And she reported that he had also played the preceding love scene in this way. Chekhov was horrified. He answered:

You write that, in this scene, Astrov turns to Yelena like a passionate lover—"He holds on to his emotion like a drowning man to a straw." But that is wrong, all wrong! Astrov likes Yelena, he is attracted by her beauty. But in the last act he knows very well that nothing will come of it, that Yelena will disappear from his life, and he speaks in this scene in the same tone he uses when talking of the heat in Africa. He kisses her merely to while away the time.

Later, Chekhov wrote directly to Stanislavsky: "Astrov whistles, you see. He whistles. Uncle Vanya weeps, but Astrov whistles." After this Stanislavsky (and it indeed speaks well for him) changed his interpretation of the role. Yet this example demonstrates how right Chekhov was when he said that Stanislavsky was still seeking to present "old theater." The acting-out of silence was for Stanislavsky what once had been the old *coup de théâtre*.

Chekhov hated overexplanations; he admonished the young Meyerhold not to exaggerate in presenting the nervousness of a lonely man. "Let it be in the tone of your voice and in your eyes, but don't project it with your hands and feet. Do it with grace, with sparse, expressive gestures." On the same subject he wrote to Olga, "Most people are nervous, most of them suffer, and only a few feel acute pain. But where—on the street or in the house—do you see people nervously running back and forth and constantly clutching their heads?"

The word "grace" is curious and noteworthy. This is how Chekhov defined what he meant by the word "grace": "When a person performing a particular action uses a minimum of movement—that is grace."

The silence Chekhov prescribes is exactly the opposite of "the acting out of silence." It is nothing other than silence, motionlessness, concentration. The Japanese actors of the *No* theater have developed this art of "doing nothing" to its highest level. Chekhov surely never saw them. But for many years he had studied actors on the stage, and he knew how much they were able to say when they were silent. He had seen Eleonora Duse; and perhaps Yermolova, too, had done similar acting. He knew how ambiguous spoken words could be. He fashioned his dialogue with this in mind. His dialogue consists of what is said and what is not said (perhaps what cannot be said).

People have counted how often the word "pause" appears in Chekhov's stage directions. Yet such a count can only be superficial; the number of pauses in Chekhov is far greater than the overt instructions indicate. The pauses occur when the actor is walking or making gestures or emptily chattering away. Chekhov's "pauses" demand of the actor the highest degree of concentration, absolute motionlessness, a distillation of thoughts and emotions in which the character is to be immersed.

Stanislavsky's use of sound effects in the stagings of Chekhov's plays has become famous. In a play that was set on a summer afternoon in the country, the theatergoer himself was to experience the illusion that he himself was spending a summer afternoon in the country. And this is how Stanislavsky justified the innumerable details with which he elaborated Chekhov's stage directions.

Certainly, Chekhov's plays require more sound effects than were ever used before on the stage. However, the sound effects Chekhov prescribes are not illusion-creating but dramaturgic. They are not there to provide mood and atmosphere—they are there to "speak." By means of the Chopin waltz Treplev plays backstage in the last act of *The Sea Gull*, he is present on the stage—giving his commentary on the dialogue. The strange sound that is twice called for in *The Cherry Orchard* tears at one's nerves. It is, as Meyerhold has said, "symbolic," so far as the assonance to the "tearing of a string" [of a violin] is to be taken literally. It is part of the elements of a theater whose effects, exactly calculated, are chosen from all the possibilities available to the stage. This sound effect does not occur "by chance"; it is not an imitation of reality. It is part of a thought-out plan in a work of art, in which chance only exists when it is intended, in which everything superfluous has been eliminated.

As there must be no misunderstanding of Chekhov's concept and use of "mood" and "atmosphere," so there must be no misunderstanding of his concept and use of "simplicity," which is so prominent and important in his observations. He criticized the verbal "extravagance" of Gorky. "Strike out all adjectives . . . ," he said to him. "Write 'The man sat down in the grass.' Basta." Chekhov's simplicity is not the language of the "simple man"; it is, like his silence, a distillation.

Chekhov once wrote to the critic Menshikov apropos one of his articles: "There is something missing in your article. You have given too little space to the character of language. It is important for your readers to know why a primitive man or a madman will use only one or two hundred words, while a Shakespeare can make use of tens of thousands."

Gorky wrote to Chekhov, observing that his language had a "magical quality, both terse and powerful." Gorky also said that Pushkin, Turgenev, and Chekhov created the Russian language.

The art of Chekhov's language lies in its terseness and brevity—"The art of writing consists less in good writing than in cutting out what is bad writing." As he so often said, everything superfluous has to be cut out. When Olga wrote to him that she was coming to grips with a monologue in *The Three Sisters*, he cabled her, "Omit everything except one sentence: 'A woman is a woman.'" When the superfluous was cut away, what emerged was not naturalism but art.

His contemporaries, Stanislavsky among them, began early to perceive the musical quality of his dialogue. As Chekhov wrote to a woman writer, everything depends on the construction of the sentence. "One must take care," he added, that it be musical." This musicalness is neither romantic nor sentimental. He hated prose that sounded like "poetry." And the always low-keyed tone in which the actors of the Moscow Art Theater spoke their lines got on his nerves. Like music, there is contrast in speech: there is forte, piano, diminuendo and crescendo, accelerando, ritardando and rubato. Whole scenes are as tightened and unified as one single bow and have to be played as such, while others are divided into exactly delineated, carefully composed parts. Pauses are parts of the composition—they are its fermatas and caesuras. Chekhov's plays have to be performed like musical compositions. (This was a goal that Stanislavsky, according to the report of his students, also set himself in his later years.)

Chekhov's structures are so terse and severe that any tampering will shake their frame. Just as Stanislavsky failed because he padded out these concentrated forms, so modern directors have failed because of their rearrangements and deletions. When Chekhov said, "It is all written down in the text," he meant not only that nothing should be staged that was not written down, but also that nothing should be left out that was written down. How could he have reproached Gorky for understanding nothing of the architecture of writing, if he had not known so exactly what meaning good architecture has for a play?

The only material of which Chekhov's plays are built are life and truth. "In art, only in art," he used to say, "one cannot lie." The plan he set himself when he wrote *Platonov*, which developed in opposition to both the idealistic and the conventional theatrical styles, culminated in bringing onto the stage an "encyclopedia of life"—as he said at the time, of Russian life. Even in his later years he did not think it possible that his plays could be performed outside Russia. It is absurd to maintain that he wished to present a naturalistic picture of his epoch (Ehrenburg commented on this refreshingly and clarifyingly), but it is equally absurd to assume that he wanted to bring the whole of Russia onto the stage. His was quite a different kind of material—and material that he knew exactly. When he criticized Tolstoy for being "ignorant," his argument was that Tolstoy wrote about syphilis while not knowing anything about how and what syphilis was. Behind the Russian foreground Chekhov presented the quintessence of all human life. Thomas Mann spoke of his uncanny gift for identifying himself with other human beings, for putting himself into their situations and condition. The writer Alexander Kuprin, who knew him well, said, "He saw and heard while looking into a person's face, hearing his voice, watching his walk, that which was hidden." Out of all this grew an "amalgam of personal observations and feelings, and of his experiences, his conjectures, and his power of imagination" (Ehrenburg).

Chekhov took over nothing exactly as he found it in life. He detested both subjectivism and naturalism. The art of composition for him boiled down to what he called his "encyclopedia," which he brought onto the stage in sparse and concentrated form. His models were Shakespeare, Cervantes, and Pushkin. *Platonov* got out of hand because the young Chekhov lacked the experience and mastery of so concentrating his material. In the next plays he was to write—*Ivanov* and *The Wood Demon* (out of which *Uncle Vanya* was to emerge)—he made up for this youthful lack of experience with concessions to the contemporary conventional theater's "dramatic" demands for "melodramatic" effect-filled scenes.

Finally, in *The Sea Gull* he succeeded in wringing out of his "encyclopedic" intention the conciseness that his vision demanded. He knew that the images that now emerged were truly art. Through distillation he shaped the rambling and accidental in true life into a form that enabled him to project the quintessence of life's truth. He let it show through the nonexisting fourth wall of the stage, so that the audience could see and recognize it. So the quintessence was brought before the audience, the jury that had to reach its verdict. Chekhov's theater, then, is one of showing, exposing.

Nothing is to be omitted if the encyclopedia is to be complete. Not illness, not chance, not dirt ("To the chemist nothing is dirty, the writer must be just as objective as the chemist"). The method of Chekhov's art was like that of a science, whose goal is the exact, precise, and subtle presentation of truth. He stayed cool as he wrote, though he loved the material with which he worked: human beings and life.

Whatever is said about Chekhov must be said in contradictions. He was a physician, yet he was also a patient and seriously ill. He "laughed through tears," as Gorky said. He wrote comedies, and they were played like tragedies. He looked through the manner and pretensions of his time and knew, and hoped, that everything was going to be different in the future, everything except that which no one can change: nature, the nature of mankind, and the nature of life.

In 1933 Gorky wrote of him:

> He had such tired hands; when they touched things, they often seemed half reluctant, half unsure. This was also the quality of his walk. He moved like a doctor in a hospital in which there are many patients but no medicines—a doctor who is not really convinced that the patients should be cured.

PLAYS

Platonov

Platonov is the work of genius of a twenty-year-old who set himself a most ambitious goal: to put on the stage an encyclopedia of Russian life. The theme, the characters, and a good deal of the dialogue foreshadow Chekhov's later masterpieces. The play's weaknesses flow from its excesses, its arbitrariness, its lack of experience. Yet, despite them it has proved itself on the stage.

In *Platonov* Chekhov collected a menagerie of characters. Everyone of these figures has his own individual psychological motivation. The action takes place on one of the innumerable Russian country estates; the time is the present (it was written between 1881 and 1884). It was a period in which many members of the nobility were deeply in debt to the bourgeoisie, when the intelligentsia, though still mired in the heritage of romanticism, was beginning to discuss radical ideas, and when the common people were starting to grumble.

Many of the play's adapters have omitted the first act. It is true that almost nothing happens during that act, yet it provides the essential background for an understanding of the play. It shows what life is like before an event occurs, an event that does not seem to be of great consequence but will bring about great changes.

The menagerie: mother and son; father, son, and daughter; fathers and sons; some rich and some debt-ridden landowners. There are: the widow of a general and a colonel; two bourgeois capitalists; former students and young people still at school; a doctor; a teacher; the common people—flunkeys and servants; a very minor civil servant; a tramp. Among these characters, there are all types of women: a desirable lady (a widow); a young, rich, buxom heiress; a dumb, poor little thing; a determined intellectual.

They all gather in the manor house of the decaying and debt-ridden Voynitsev estate (it belongs to the general's widow) to open the social season after the long winter. They have not seen each other for a long time. What have they been doing all these months? Some of them have been in town, others have "put on fat." One of them got married and his wife is still "new." Everything is just as it has always been at this time of year, when winter is over. As always, there are the conversations about life, money, women, the good old and the bad new times, affairs, scandals. Again, there will be more conversations, affairs, scandals, and perhaps some of the secret excesses which everyone knows about. The next day everything will be again as it has always been. Summer will pass, they will grow older, and the next spring they will see each other again and begin a new season, and its course will be the same as that of the season one is now experiencing: ennui, boredom, emptiness. . . .

The general's widow and the doctor, while awaiting the arrival of the rest of the company, are playing chess. They talk about, yet conceal, what they are thinking about. The doctor loves the young, rich mistress of the neighboring estate, but he knows that she is in love with his friend Platonov, who, everyone says, is having an affair with the general's widow.

The first arrival is a landowner, a count of an old aristocratic family, a man completely of the "grand old days," a romantic and cavalier of yesterday who has today's real money. He is courting the general's widow, and it is no secret why he has a chance of winning her. Her estate will be saved if she marries him, for he then will pay her debts. Later Platonov appears, an aristocrat who lost his estate and now earns his living as the village schoolteacher (he had studied at the university but had not taken his degree). With him enters Sasha, his wife, who is the doctor's sister, wearing Russian dress—the poor little thing with the heart of gold who adores her husband.

The dramatic event slowly goes in motion. The son of the general's widow—who says of himself that he is "sick, effeminate, limited, and sentimental," who has gotten his degree and is a secondary-school teacher—is going to introduce his young wife Sofia to the company. He has brought her to the estate from Moscow for the first time. She will soon be returning from a walk. But before her return another representative of the older generation arrives—a retired colonel, the father of the doctor and of Mrs. Platonov, a vain, sentimental old duffer. Other guests arrive; two Jewish moneylenders, one of them with his son, a student who expounds his radical views. The last arrival is the rich young mistress of the neighboring estate. She immediately quarrels with Platonov, who behaves toward her with his usual insolence.

Platonov is a Don Juan in the country. He has had some kind of relationship with each of these women.

Women pursue him because he has a "good-looking mug" and is brighter than the rest of the company. His pose is that of a melancholic cynic, and his vanity is as great as his disgust with himself. He ruined and lost his estate, gave up his studies, and made a shameless compromise in the way he now lives. Yet he is deeply attached to his wife who takes care of him, and their child. Platonov teaches the peasant children, and, when the social season begins, he plays the roles in which he likes to see himself: Don Juan, Hamlet, the court's fool, philosopher, conversationalist.

Sofia's entrance sparks the dramatic action. Five years ago, she and Platonov shared a great love. Now, however, she hardly recognizes him. But the tension between the two makes it clear that nothing is forgotten.

Yet the social life continues. Two more characters enter—a rich land-owning neighbor, (also, of course, a creditor), and the count's son, an arrogant spendthrift who has just returned from Paris because his father had stopped sending him money. The guests move to the salon, where a meal is about to be served, and Platonov leads Sofia to the table.

I have described this scene in such detail to show how Chekhov constructs its tensions. In two brief episodes the groundwork is laid for all that is to happen. In one the creditor, alone with the general's widow, explains to her that he will not honor the bad checks she has given him: she will have to pay up or sell the estate. In the other a tramp suddenly stands at the door. They all know him. It is barefooted Ossip, who has joined the ranks of the poor, a Tolstoy figure—no, rather a Gorky character (though Gorky had not begun to write at this time), albeit drawn with Chekhov's ironic skepticism. We find out that the general's widow once, in a jest, condescended to

let him kiss her, and that since then he loves her,
abjectly, with a dog's love. He allows himself to be
bribed to play a prank on Platonov to teach him a
lesson. Ossip takes the money; but, later, before at-
tacking Platonov, he throws it away, for by then he
has seen Platonov with the general's widow and is
consumed with jealousy.

The action of the second act takes place a few
days later, on Midsummer Night. Under the smooth
surface, the various aggressions have become sharper.
The scene is the garden of the Voynitsev estate
illuminated by party lanterns. There is dancing in the
house. Drunken guests come out, some play hide-and-
seek, pair off, and disappear. Platonov is in his element. His wife, repelled by all this drunkenness, goes
home. She knows how things are; she will wait for
him. He will come home when he has had enough.

There are scenes showing Platonov with the various
women: with the rich young heiress, who runs away
crying because he has taunted her again; with the
general's widow, who sees through him yet wants
him as he is, and presses him for a decision; with
Sofia, whom he provokes by reviling her husband.
Sofia's "purity and honesty" attract him irresistibly; he
feels that she has brought back the days of his youth,
when he still had faith: "If I only had the strength to
pull her and myself out of this mire! Life! Why can't
we live as well as we are able to?" Sofia is bewildered: "Either he is the messenger of a new life or he
will destroy me."

Meanwhile macabre events are taking place. The
young count, urged on by the ironic Platonov who
told him that he could succeed, proposes to the general's widow, vulgarly drawing out his wallet as he
does so. She throws him out. But he tells his father
the opposite—that she kissed him and that they dis-

cussed the marriage terms. The old man, who hoped that she would become his wife, is so deeply shaken that he has a stroke. Other masks fall, too, and it becomes evident that the ruin of the estate can no longer be averted.

The third act, which follows without a time lapse, takes place in front of the schoolhouse, at the edge of a forest. Telegraph lines and train rails glisten in the moonlight. (Chekhov once said that a gun, leaning against a wall of the stage, tells the audience that eventually it will go off; this, similarly, could be said of these train rails.) Now melodramatic, even bizarre scenes follow one upon another. Secrets are overheard. Drunks stagger, apparently accidentally, across the stage. Violent quarrels occur that seem motivated less by the necessities of life than by the artistic needs of the young author. Platonov comes home. His wife has stayed up to wait for him. They embrace; he is moved and calls himself a cad. But before he can walk into the house, the general's widow appears, in riding dress.

The general's widow wants him to come away with her: "Chase the demons away, let us live!" He promises to come to her, but other encounters follow and change his intentions. Finally, a maid from the Voynitsev manor house brings him a letter from Sofia: "I am making the first step. Come, let us begin a new life. I await you at four o'clock." Platonov ruminates aloud. Ruin a marriage? Yet, could this not be happiness? Then, again, drunks turn up, among them Sofia's husband, who is carrying a rifle. They ask Platonov to come along on a hunt. He rushes away.

An approaching train is heard in the distance. Ossip the tramp now runs onto the stage. (He had appeared in the first scene of this act, and Platonov's

Platonov. Produced at the Piccolo Teatro, Milan, in 1959. Directed by Giorgio Strehler. Stage sets by Luciano Damiani.

Platonov, which did not come to light until after Chekhov's death, found its true interpreter in Giorgio Strehler, who produced it after publishing an Italian translation of it. This scene shows Tino Buazzelli (who played the philandering Platonov) with Sarah Ferrati.
PICCOLO TEATRO DI MILANO

Ivanov. Produced at the Shubert Theater, New York City, in 1966. Directed by John Gielgud.

Ivanov (as played by John Gielgud), an ineffectual intellectual, is watched yearningly by his ill wife, Anna Petrovna (as played by Vivien Leigh). This role in the rarely performed *Ivanov* was Vivien Leigh's last New York performance before her death.

FRIEDMAN–ABELES

Uncle Vanya. Produced at the Old Vic Theatre, London, in 1962. Directed by Lawrence Olivier.

The major Chekhov roles have long been the favorites of distinguished actors. In this scene Uncle Vanya (as played by Michael Redgrave) allows himself to be comforted by his niece Sonya (as played by Joan Plowright).

The Sea Gull. Produced by the Theater Guild, New York City, in 1938.

Here the aging actress Arkadina (as played by Lynn Fontanne) acts the great scene of her life when her lover Trigorin (as played by Alfred Lunt) begs her to let him go.

CULVER PICTURES, INC.

The Sea Gull. Produced at the Royal Dramaten Theater, Stockholm, in 1961. Directed by Ingmar Bergman.

Ingmar Bergman is among the contemporary theater
people who are reaching toward new goals in the
staging of Chekhov's plays. This scene shows Nina
(as played by Christina Schollin), holding the dead
sea gull, and Konstantin Treplev (as played by Per
Myberg), the young writer who loves her to no avail.

The Three Sisters. Produced at the Barrymore Theater, New York City, in 1943. Directed by Guthrie McClintic.

In this all-star production, Irina (left) was played by Gertrude Musgrove, Olga (center) by Judith Anderson, Masha (right) by Katherine Cornell, and Natasha, the domineering sister-in-law (not shown here), by Ruth Gordon.

The Three Sisters. Produced at the Württembergisches Staatstheater, Stuttgart, in 1965. Directed by Rudolf Noelte.

In the last decade theater people have been seeking to throw off the influence of Stanislavsky on the production of Chekhov. One of the successful new interpretations is this of Rudolf Noelte. The three sisters are played by Elisabeth Schwarz (as Masha), Cordula Trantow (as Irina), and Elisabeth Müller (as Olga).

MADELINE WINKLER-BETZENDAHL

The Cherry Orchard. Produced at the Württembergisches Staatstheater, Stuttgart, in 1968. Directed by
Peter Zadek. Stage design by Wilfried Minks.

Peter Zadek, another of the new interpreters of
Chekhov, took seriously Chekhov's feeling that Stanislavsky "had ruined" this play. In this 1968 production
he stressed the coolness and cruelty of Chekhov's
vision. This scene shows Gaev (as played by Günther
Lüders) and Andreyevna Ranevskaya (as played by
Edith Heerdegen).

wife fed him.) Ossip is wild with jealousy. He had seen Platonov with the general's widow and is now looking for him to take his revenge. As Platonov is not here, Ossip assumes that he must be with her. The unhappy wife, who has come out of the house in nightgown and bedjacket and heard Ossip's revelation, wants to throw herself under the oncoming train. She is saved by the tramp.

The action of Act IV takes place three weeks later. The scene is Platonov's room, in the school house, in great disorder. Platonov is sleeping on a sofa. His wife has left him. Sofia arrives from the manor house and wakes him. She has taken the second step, too: her husband knows everything. She wants Platonov to go away with her, and he is faced with a decision: does he really want to go with her and begin a new life? He gives her his word: "We shall leave and earn our bread by the sweat of our brow."

But Sophia barely leaves before his indecision returns. A bailiff enters, very realistically portrayed, and brings him a summons. The rich young heiress has brought charges against him; she has asked for his dismissal or, at least, for his disciplinary transfer. But this doesn't disturb Platonov; he knows how to treat women. He sends her the summons, on which he has written, "Today I shall kiss you as I would a saint."

More difficult is the liaison with the general's widow, who now appears. He tells her that he will be going away. She assumes that he is going alone and says, "I don't believe you are capable of anything so serious." They proceed to have a drink together. The general's widow now unmasks herself: "I am a secret drinker, Platonov, and have been for a long time. There is nothing worse than a mature, intelligent woman without anything to do, without a reason for living. For what am I living? To whom am I of any importance? I am an amoral woman. [Laughing:] Amoral, against my will. Yes, I am an amoral woman. And that is probably exactly why I love you. I am amoral. I am superfluous, completely superfluous." She proposes that she come along and that they make the journey together. "If you go, then go with me." Then she leaves.

Platonov, now alone, thinks he has found a solution. He will first travel with the general's widow, then leave her to lead a new life with Sofia. While he thinks over these intriguing possibilities, Ossip the tramp appears at the door. He has come to kill Platonov. There is a struggle. Platonov's wife enters just as Ossip draws his knife, and she throws herself between the two men. She has returned to ask Platonov to come to their child, who is deathly ill. The tramp leaves, and Platonov begs his wife's forgiveness. He tells her simply that he cannot live without her, and, at that moment, he is probably perfectly sincere. But, thinking aloud, he gives himself away and lets her know that he is not only involved with the general's widow but with Sofia, too—a married woman! Weeping, his wife, Sasha, tears herself away from him.

Sofia's husband enters and challenges Platonov to a duel. "I will shoot myself," Platonov cries out, "I swear I will shoot myself!"

The last act again takes place at the Voynitsev manor house. Now everything comes to a head. The duel did not take place. And Ossip the tramp no longer threatens to kill Platonov; he was beaten to death by peasants. Platonov has not gone away. The general's widow's estate is lost, for the count, who had recovered from his stroke, was not present at its auction; he and his son had gone off to Paris.

The time is late morning, on a dark day. A driving

rain is beating against the windows. The scene takes place in the general's old study. Besides a rifle case, collections of rifles, sabers, and pistols line the walls. Sofia has just sent the maid to Platonov, who again has broken his word; he can't be found. The general's widow learns from her son that Sofia wants to leave him for Platonov, and she is determined to take Platonov to task. "One has to save what can be saved," she says. The young heiress comes to call. She is in despair because Platonov really is being transferred to another post. Then Platonov himself staggers in, his arm in a sling. He looks tired, unkempt, feverish. The doctor is called and arrives bringing bad news: his sister, Platonov's wife, has made a gruesome suicide attempt. Platonov collapses: "A thousand Platonovs aren't worth one Sasha. . . . Who is worth living in this world if not she?" But when the doctor tells him that she will be saved, Platonov embraces him, and laughs, "I have never believed in medicine, but now I believe even in you!" Sofia becomes hysterical and is led away.

Platonov, left alone in the room, groans, "I must go to Sasha!" But he doesn't have the strength. He takes a pistol from the desk drawer and puts it against his temple; but he cannot shoot—"Isn't there anybody who will kill me?" Now the young heiress enters; "Come," she says. "Everything is all right. My carriage is waiting downstairs." Half-feverish, he again begins his usual routine—"They are all in love with me. When I'm well again, I'll seduce her." Unobserved, Sofia has entered the room, in time to see them kiss. She takes the pistol and shoots Platonov. The bullet hits his chest. He stares at her, surprised: "Sofia. . . . Why? . . ." He falls to the floor, as they all run into the room. The doctor pronounces him dead.

Chekhov, as I said earlier, did not succeed in inter-

esting a theater in the *Platonov* play. In 1920 a
heavily edited draft of it, in a folder on which was
written "Play without a Title," was found among
Chekhov's papers when they were transferred from
the family's ownership to the Soviet state archives.
The play was first published in 1923, but only people
in the field of literature and literary history paid any
attention to its publication. And then, when the Soviet state publishing house printed Chekhov's collected works (1944-51), *Platonov* was included
(volume twelve). In 1952, an English adaptation appeared, entitled *Don Juan in the Russian Manner*.
In 1956, a French adaptation by Pol Quentin, entitled *Ce fou de Platonov*, was produced by Jean
Vilar at the Festival de Bordeaux. This extensive
adaptation has been widely performed. The vitality
of the original play is most effectively communicated
in the Milan production of Giorgio Strehler, for which
he used the Italian translation he published in col-
laboration with Ettore Lo Gatto. It follows the original text closely and is entitled *Platonov e Altri*. The
German translation, by Otto Mueller, is called simply
Platonov.

While at work on *Platonov*, or shortly before—
sometime between 1877 and 1881—Chekhov wrote
another full-length play, entitled "Without Fathers,"
which is not extant.

Ivanov

In the fall of 1887, in a period of eleven days, Chekhov wrote the first version of *Ivanov*. He wrote the play to prove to his friends in the theater that he could write an ordinary play—a "normal" play —as the conventional theater required it, effortlessly and, "with his left hand." The theater director Korsh had pressed him to write a play, trying to convince him that he should play, as in his stories, "upon the nerves of his audience."

Chekhov invented a plot with melodramatic tensions and, literally, with explosive effects. But, as he said over and over again, he could work only with material based on his experiences and memories (on what he knew well). And so the scenes, the dialogue, and especially the conception of the characters were infused with truth and reality. He admitted that his major incentive had been the wish to earn a thousand rubles. Yet he also admitted that his characters "were not made of sea foam and bubbles, or of preconceived ideas, or by accident: they were the result of observations, of my study of life as it is. They are in my head, and I feel that not an inch of this is lie, and not an iota, exaggeration." He wrote these words while the Saint Petersburg production (1888) was in preparation. A triumphant success, it was to make up for the flop of the earlier Moscow premiere (at the Korsh Theater in 1887). Yet Chekhov believed that the play was a failure. One cannot contradict him; the discrepancy between the truth of the material and the calculated splashy effects of the plot cannot be bridged.

The plot: Ivanov, a landowner, deeply in debt, is now only the wreck of the vigorous man he once was. He is a frustrated intellectual, revolted by the emptiness of his present life and wallowing in self-pity. He is married to a Jewish woman who is now extremely ill with tuberculosis. She is not told what her husband and her doctor know: she does not have long to live. Every night, a kind of claustrophobia drives Ivanov to leave his house and visit the rich Lebedevs, the owners of the neighboring estate to whom he is so deeply in debt that they have him in their power. When they insist (really Mrs. Lebedev, who controls the household and the money) that he pay his debt, which is due, he faces ruin. In the Lebedev household, there is a young daughter who is in love with Ivanov and is determined to save him from his misery. At the end of the first act, Ivanov's wife (who has converted to Christianity and is now called Anna Petrovna instead of Sarah) is left alone by Ivanov who is visiting the Lebedevs. She convinces her young doctor, who thinks she is a saint and hates her husband, to drive her to the Lebedevs. At the end of the second act, at the Lebedevs, she comes upon Ivanov and the young girl. "Sarah!" Ivanov cries out, horrified, which hits her like a slap.

The anti-Semitic background for the play must be taken seriously: the young Chekhov had witnessed the deportation of 20,000 Jews from Moscow. The people say, of course, that Ivanov married his Jewish wife for her money, and they gloat over the fact that her family renounced her when she changed her religion because of her love for Ivanov. One should keep in mind that Ivanov, when he married her, had the inner strength to surmount the prejudices and gossiping of his society. But that same Ivanov, by the end of the third act, screams at his deathly ill wife. "Be quiet . . . Jewess!" It is the hopelessness of his situation that drives him to this excess of cruelty. He simply is no longer in his right mind as he gets further worked up and screams, "You're going to die soon!" And the border of the absurd is reached when he clutches his head and screams, "Oh my God, how guilty I am!"

Nevertheless, he is not as guilty as his wife assumes, who sees the girl riding toward the house, but does not know that she is coming against Ivanov's will: "Your coming will have a dreadful effect upon my wife. . . . She is near death."

A year passes between the action of the third and the fourth act. Sarah is dead. On the estate of the Lebedevs they are preparing for the wedding of Ivanov and the young heiress. Again there is gossiping and whispering among the menagerie of characters with which Chekhov has surrounded Ivanov to explain Ivanov's loathing of the milieu in which he is living. Ivanov and his bride have an open talk, and it becomes clear that they both now think the whole thing is a comedy. (As Ivanov can no longer be "saved," the girl is now tired of his constant complaining.) But the family, fearing a scandal, insists that the wedding take place. Ivanov is determined not to let it come to pass. At this moment the young doctor enters, the personification of integrity, and, agreeing with the judgment of everyone, he calls Ivanov a scoundrel. The girl unmasks this honorable man, accusing him of being driven by hate of Ivanov.

But Ivanov himself breaks into laughter. "This isn't a wedding," he says, "it's a parliamentary session!" He runs out of the room. From backstage we hear a shot.

This is a melodramatic *coup de théâtre*, for at the beginning of the play, a shot almost goes off. At the beginning of the first act, music is heard from the house (a cello and a piano), while Ivanov sits at a table in the garden, reading a book. Suddenly, the drunken manager of Ivanov's estate appears, a miserable cynic and therefore a sought-after salon lion, and aims a rifle at the frightened Ivanov—a joke.

As a "normal" play had to have a hero, Chekhov chose Ivanov. It is a character-tragicomedy or, better, a character-comitragedy. In this hero the Russian intelligentsia was supposed to recognize itself. Ivanov's state is not merely the result of his milieu and his circumstances but also the result of a process that most men pass through when their youth is past and they begin to age. Besides, it is also an individual Ivanov-process, rooted in Ivanov's character and in his reaction to his particular situation and to the general human condition. Chekhov said that he had first intended to call him Ivan Ivanovich Ivanov, to accentuate the typical in the character. But Chekhov did not succeed in holding himself down to creating a merely typical intellectual.

Chekhov wrote about Ivanov in a letter to Suvorin. This was the only time that he commented in such detail on one of his plays:

> His past is excellent and distinguished, as in the case of so many Russian intellectuals. . . . Their present condition is always worse than the past. Why? Because the Russian excitability has a specific quality: it soon gives way to tiredness. . . . He feels physical exhaustion and emptiness,

but he does not understand what is the matter with him. . . . The change he sees in himself offends his feeling of decency. He looks for the reasons outside and cannot discover them. And so he begins to look for them in himself and finds only an indefinite feeling of guilt. This feeling is truly Russian. The Russian always feels guilty—when someone in his family gets sick or dies; if he owes someone money or lends it out himself. . . . And his enemies, tiredness and boredom, are joined by another: loneliness. If Ivanov were a civil servant, an actor, a priest, or a professor, he would be used to this condition. But he lives on a country estate. There people are either drunkards, gamblers, or, like the doctor, honorable men. None of the characters is concerned with Ivanov's emotions and what has happened to him. He is alone. Long winters, long evenings, an empty garden, empty rooms, a surly count [his uncle], a sick wife. . . . There is no journey he can make, there is nowhere for him to go. And so he is tortured every minute by the question, what then should I do? Now comes his fifth enemy: Ivanov is tired, has no insight into himself, but life goes on and makes its demands. He must, whether he wants to or not, make decisions. His sick wife is a problem, the pile of debts is a problem, the young girl Sasha is on his neck, and that is a problem too. . . . People like Ivanov don't solve problems, they break down. They lose their composure, tear out their hair, get nervous, complain and whine, do foolish things. In the end, when they finally give their sluggish, uncontrolled nerves free rein, they lose the ground under their feet. . . . I had a daring dream: to summarize everything that has ever been written about complaining, whining, and melancholic people and make a definitive end of it, terminating it all in *Ivanov*.

In some of the scenes, the dialogue achieves a virtuosity hardly equaled in any of Chekhov's other plays. Undoubtedly, working within the structural laws of the "well-made play" enriched his experience in the "construction" and "building" of a play. The path from the *Platonov* plan to the chamber-music technique of *The Sea Gull* had to lead through the writing of *Ivanov*—and also through the writing of *The Wood Demon* and the revising of that into *Uncle Vanya*.

The Wood Demon
AND
Uncle Vanya

Because the transforming of *The Wood Demon* into *Uncle Vanya* is so illuminating of Chekhov's development as a dramatist, far more so than can be demonstrated in the scope of this book, we shall handle these two plays together although *Uncle Vanya* was written after *The Sea Gull*.

Shortly after writing *Ivanov*, Chekhov planned out a play that was to compensate himself and others for the concessions he had made in *Ivanov* to the conventional theater. He worked for a long time on this new play, which was to be *The Wood Demon*. He said it was "a lengthy comedy, a sort of novel," and that, "from the beginning to the end, the tone is lyrical." Later, he added the subtitle *Scenes from Country Life*, for here he had returned to his *Platonov* plan. Yet, this work was more. The kind of action treated in *Ivanov* now was added to the earlier "encyclopedia of country life," and it was all heightened by the presence of an idea. This is the only one among Chekhov's plays in which something resembling a "message" is intimated. This message is rooted in Tolstoyism, in which he was involved at the time, which later was reason enough for him to hate the play. After the Imperial Maly Theater had rejected it, ostensibly for artistic reasons, it was produced, under the title *Leshy*, in December 1889 at a private theater in Moscow. It did not please the audience.

Chekhov withdrew it at once and later did not include it when he collected his works for publication. But he was attached to the characters he had brought together in the play. When he finished work on *The Sea Gull*, he again returned to the manuscript. Now, seven years later, years in which he had traveled to Sakhalin and made his complete break with Tolstoyism, he was drawn back to revise *The Wood Demon*.

He now took out everything that displeased him; primarily, the idea, but also the fusion of a plot in the *Ivanov* manner with the *Platonov* plan. The experience he had gained in writing *The Sea Gull* now enabled him to work out his previous "encyclopedic" plan by means of a simple course of action. *Uncle Vanya*, which now emerged, was published in 1897, but was not produced until 1899, when it had its premiere at the Moscow Art Theater. The style of the play is neither lyrical nor that of a "comedy-novel." Gorky called it "an intensely original, incomparable play," and "a completely new kind of dramatic art." The play has held its own along with Chekhov's three masterpieces: *The Sea Gull*; *The Three Sisters*; *The Cherry Orchard*.

The Wood Demon was called *Leshy* in Russian. Translated into French, this should be *Le Sylvain*—literally, "he who lives in the woods." The French translators, however, preferred to call the play *Le Sauvage*—"the wild one." The English title, *The Wood Demon*, is supposed to mean not a demon or a creature of the spirit world, but a man who lives "in the spirit of the woods" and who tries to defend them against the "spirit of destruction" that is preying on modern society. "Woods make the world beautiful and teach mankind to understand beauty. It is barbaric to destroy them for commercial gain. For so the dwelling places of the animals are destroyed, the rivers run dry, the climate deteriorates, and with every day the earth becomes poorer and uglier."

The "wood demon," Mikhail Khrushchov, does not simply live in the forest. He fights, wherever he can, against the destructive tree-chopping that is going on.

> When I pass the peasants' forests I have saved from the ax, and when I hear the rustling of the leaves in the trees I planted with my own hands, I feel just a little that I, too, am master over the climate, and when in a thousand years mankind will be happier than it is now, I, too, will have a share in it.

This man of the woods would not be a true Chekhov character if he lived like a primitive man in a self-chosen, romantic paradise— actually, he is a physician. He works, although not in ecstasy, from early in the morning until late into the night. The peasants revere him like a hero, even a saint. To them he is a higher being. Society, however, especially aristocratic society, treats him with contempt, although it avails itself of his medical service. To the aristocrats he is a "democrat." But in the ladies this unusual man seems to kindle a great attraction, which brings confusion into the country society.

The most important change Chekhov made when he reworked *The Wood Demon* into *Uncle Vanya* was to abandon this character, who is so reminiscent of Tolstoy's teaching. Like Tolstoy, the great prophet of love for his fellowmen, he wears a peasant blouse, even when he appears in society. The excision of the woodsman was accompanied by the elimination of the programmatic idea of the play, a considerable part of the action, and a number of characters. Removed also is the aspect of the structure that projected the idea—the forest pitted against society, the spirit of goodness and beauty pitted against the spirit of destruction.

The society that confronts Mikhail Khrushchov—who is also an aristocrat and a landowner—is made up of two different social circles. Included in the first are the landowners and their wives, each of which is individualized by the differences of their interests. There is a menagerie of realists, blockheads, and parasites, some of whom, however, are not adverse to thinking. In the second, there are the members of the intelligentsia whom fate has thrown into country society. These are the most interesting.

Their center is Professor Serebryakov, a great luminary of science and literature. Now retired, he has come to live in the country with his second wife, Yelena. With them is his first wife's mother, who idolizes him. It is on her estate that they are now living. The professor is a cold egotist who tyrannizes the family with his various illnesses and moods. When his fame was in its zenith, he had been quite a Don Juan. Yelena, a gifted young pianist, had succumbed to the glamour of that fame. But here in the country the glamour has quickly paled, and Yelena, too, is beginning to recognize what the "great man" is really like.

There are two characters who have dedicated their lives to serve the professor, the pride of their family —the daughter and the brother, Voynitsky, of the professor's first wife. These two (who will become Sonya and Uncle Vanya in *Uncle Vanya*) have worked like peasants to wring out of the estate sufficient funds to support the great man in the style to which he is accustomed. Now that he lives among them, they are forced to draw the appalling conclusion: since leaving the city, his fame, his eminence are gone, burst like a bubble. "Not a single page of his work will survive him. He is nothing! We have been miserably deceived!" The fraud is exposed. But nothing will convince him to give up his claims and pretension. Not only does he continue to play his accustomed role of grandeur but he also suffers because here in the country he withers away like an exile; he craves acclaim and fame, or, as he once says, "a dozen ladies to idolize me."

In the manor house, which had once been imbued with a spirit of work and dedication, "the spirit of destruction" now reigns. Its members hate each other. The hour comes when the masks fall. The arrogant and ruthless Serebryakov announces that he intends to sell the estate (although he isn't really its owner!) in order to buy a villa in Finland (near the Russian capital, Saint Petersburg), where he plans to live with his wife. This brings about an accounting and an open break. Voynitsky, who is unhappily in love with Yelena, sees himself cast aside like a dog. He now confronts the great man with the truth: "For us you have always been a higher being. But all your works aren't worth a kopeck! You have made fools of us, deceived us. . . . You've ruined my life. You have robbed me of the best years of my life." Then Yelena screams, "I won't stay another minute in this hell!" Voynitsky runs out of the room and, while the women try to quiet the professor, a shot is heard. Voynitsky has killed himself.

But this could not be the ending of *The Wood Demon*, whose hero was Khrushchov, not Voynitksy. The shot follows upon a love scene between Yelena and Khrushchov, in which she implores the "demon" to believe in the sincerity of her feelings. He exclaims brusquely and with revulsion: "I despise your friendship!" Yelena, in despair, calls after Khrushchov, "But why? Why?" And after the shot goes off, she repeats the same words. "Why? Why?"

The last act of *The Wood Demon* takes place two weeks later, in the forest, before a house by the mill. Yelena, who has left her husband, is now staying here, at the home of one of Khrushchov's friends, while waiting for money that will enable her to return to Moscow. In this scene Chekhov brings together the same menagerie of characters we have seen in the first act—for a picnic. They have decided not to speak about Voynitsky's death any more. But this cannot be done so simply. Not with Khrushchov there, who has been deeply wrought up by the suicide of his friend Voynitsky.

"We say that we serve mankind, and at the same time we inflict deadly wounds upon each other. What did we do to save him? Where is your peace? Everything is lost, destroyed, gone up in smoke. . . . My friends call me the demon, but I am not the only one; in each of us there is a demon. You all are lost in the woods, you all live in darkness. . . . Until now I have believed that I am a human being with ideas, a creature who loves his fellowman—yet I can't forgive those who are dearest to me the slightest fault. I believed in lies, and I have slandered just like the others, and when your wife trustingly offered me her friendship, I answered her from the height of my lofty grandeur 'I despise your friendship!' Yes, inside me there is a demon, I am a wretch! But you, professor, are not an iota better than I am. And all the time the whole district, and especially the women, saw in me a hero, a higher human being, and you, professor, enjoy fame throughout Russia. But when creatures like you and me are taken for true heroes, it means that there are no people of real greatness and talent, that no man can help us find our way out of this dark forest, that there is no one who will rectify our errors. . . . Yes, I am a wretch, but you, professor, are no better. And the one who could think of nothing better than to shoot a bullet through his head was a wretch, too. . . . None of us is any good. . . ."

At this moment Yelena steps forward, and, causing general confusion, announces that she has decided to stay with her husband. If the world is as Khrushchov has just described it (she seems to want to say), what sense does it make to try to change our way of life? She now comes out with her favorite line (which she will still have in the later version of the play). "I am an episodic woman." Ironically everything now falls into place. The picnic continues. Suddenly, in the background there is the blaze of a forest fire. The peasants have set fire to the woods, to win more arable land. The wood demon rushes off. "I am no hero? The devil, I'll be one!" Yelena then turns to Serebryakov, "Now, statue of the commandant, please take me home!"

Flattered, Serebryakov smiles: "I thank you all. It was a charming evening, the tea was excellent, and everything would be perfect if it weren't for your provincial philosophy and conception of life. One must work, my dear friends. That is the only way one can live. One must work! Amen!"

One can imagine how this ending irritated the audience of the Palais Theater, where the play had its premiere. How could the audience have accepted a provocation of this kind? In *Uncle Vanya*, Chekhov was to retract only slightly. The elimination of the antagonist took some of the edge from this devastating judgment of society, a society that he meant to portray as typically Russian only in some of its aspects.

The character Chekhov now put in the place of the wood demon is anything but a "hero" in the eyes of those who are around him; even he himself says that he is a questionable character. This doctor Astrov is a skeptic, posing as a man who despises mankind. He cannot fight against his emotions when he realizes that he loves the professor's wife. All he has of the wood demon are his first names. The society that confronted the wood demon is now reduced to the family of the professor, his wife, and their entourage. Four characters have disappeared from the menagerie. And only one, which indeed is very different, has been added: Marina, the old nurse; as it were, Mother Russia personified.

Although the doctor stands in the configuration where Khrushchov stood before, he does not move into the center of the plot. Voynitsky, who shot himself in the third act of the earlier play, now, as Uncle Vanya, is the hero. Now when he tries to shoot himself he misses; when he chases after the professor, to shoot him, he misses again. And so the fourth act can belong to him. This act brings the departure of the professor and Yelena. The irony of the "great man's" last words is now further sharpened by a line that is loaded with Chekhov's full wrath. Affably condescending, the callous poseur addresses Uncle Vanya, the man he has ruined: "After all that has happened, I have thought a great deal. Now, I believe, I could write an essay for posterity on the art of how to live."

There now is a last scene, between Astrov and

Yelena, in which the two finally admit what they feel
for each other.

> YELENA: We shall never see each other again,
> so why make a secret of it? I was really a little
> in love with you.
>
> ASTROV: You are a good person. And yet there
> is something strange about you. When you ar-
> rived with your husband, everyone here, who
> had been working, who had been busy, ac-
> complishing something, had to drop whatever
> he was doing and attend to your husband's
> gout. You infected us with your slothfulness. I
> have lazed away a whole month, while the
> people have grown sicker. . . . Wherever you
> and your husband go, you bring destruction.
> [He laughs.] I am joking, but if you were to
> stay here you would have a devastating effect.
> I, too, would be destroyed, and you, you
> wouldn't have much to laugh about either. So
> go away! *Finita la commedia*!

More important than the love affair is the carefully
worked-out parallel between the character of Astrov
and that of Uncle Vanya. In *Uncle Vanya* Chekhov's
characters have become more complicated and therefore more true. Uncle Vanya, whose indignation about
the professor's egotism is shared by everyone in the
audience, is unfair to the professor before the sale of
the estate is discussed, because of his reckless love for
Yelena. "It is immoral to deceive the man, yet it is
more immoral to sacrifice youth, beauty, and freedom
to such a wretch." But it is not this alone. The despair
about the hopelessness of this love changes Vanya's
consciousness of his own life. His work no longer

interests him. He begins to drink. The ideas in which
he had believed no longer seem valid to him because
they are contained in the professor's books. He can
no longer sleep at night, because he is gripped by the
panicky feeling that his life is irrevocably lost. The
present is dreadful in its absurdity. All that it takes
is an impetus—the professor's plan—to bring about
the catastrophe and have him reach for his gun.

His friend Astrov, the logical man and physician,
who can look at himself and at others more coolly,
regards his life not much differently. "My mind is
still intact, but my emotions have become dulled. . . .
Life is boring, foolish, dirty. It pulls us down into the
mud." Apart from all this there is the trauma of a
patient having died under his hands on the operating
table: "It is as if I had killed him intentionally." Facing Yelena, he suddenly believes his ideas about the
woods are paltry and that she is right when she asks,
"You strive to save the woods, but who saves the people?" And he feels that the atmosphere in the house
has become poisoned and how despite this, against
his will, he is drawn there irresistibly every day. "I
am growing older, am overworked, and I am no
longer capable of love." And he adds, "The only thing
seemingly that still attracts me is beauty." Even his
personal fight against hunger, against indolence,
seems to him suddenly suspect, and in an episode
that rings with truth it is Yelena herself who asks him
to stop coming to the house. From now on his appear-
ances are only vacillating actions, a preparation for
taking farewell forever.

In the last scene with Uncle Vanya the decisive
words are said:

> Those who are going to live a hundred or two
> hundred years after us . . . will perhaps find a

way to be happy. We two have only one hope: that when we lie in our graves we shall have pleasant dreams. Yes, my friend, in this district there were only two decent, intelligent men: you and I. But in less than ten years the morass of everyday life has swallowed us up; its foul vapors have poisoned our blood, and we have become just as petty and commonplace as all the others.

"What silence," says Astrov, after the bells of the departed coach can no longer be heard. Then he leaves too.

Uncle Vanya stays behind with Sonya. They work. And Sonya, who loves Astrov and knows that she is not loved in return, speaks the last words: "We shall rest. I believe, I believe . . . we shall rest."

In this grim irony there is now a note of the tragic. Everything will again be as it was before all this began. And everything will not be as it was before. And nothing will ever be as it should be.

The Sea Gull

In the garden of a manor house a small theater has been erected. It is evening. After the sun has set, an amateur performance will take place. The stage curtain conceals the view of the lake that is in the background. From the little theater, the hammering of unseen workers is heard. The play will be directed by its young author Konstantin Gavrilovich Treplev, who is the son of a famous actress. She is spending the summer on the estate which once has been the scene of her youth. Now the estate belongs to her brother, a high civil servant and retired civil councillor.

And so one of the major themes has been introduced: art, literature, the theater. What is to be performed on the little stage is dipped into various ironic nuances. In the last act, which takes place years later, the little "theater" will still play its role, and will be cut to shreds with ironic touches. It then stands in tatters, about to fall apart, its frame rattling in the autumn wind, a skeleton. One of the characters sensibly suggests that it ought to be torn down. But now, in the first act, it is just being built. It is summer, and a play is about to be performed. For some of the characters what they will watch will be "theater," for others it will be life, real life. In four scenes, we see pairs of characters on the stage, before they finally all assemble—the audience for the play within the play.

These scenes, lightly, almost imperceptibly hinged together, are launching the play, pressing the actors forward toward the play within the play. In these dialogues the expectations of each of the characters are outlived.

These characters are never just what they say about themselves—with one exception, and it is not by accident that this one is a doctor. We see the characters as they see themselves and also as others see them. Occasionally it is as if they are standing in a spot lit up by several different, overlapping floodlights that are turned on them.

Years before *The Sea Gull* was written Chekhov had warned angrily that he was not to be credited with the views expressed by his characters. And he had added that a dramatist is not the judge of his characters; that it is his task to present the case, and that the judgment is up to the jury—the audience. He still believed this. But now he went a step further: the characters are presented less as the dramatist sees them than as they view themselves. After seeing the dual images—how a character sees himself and how he appears to others—the "jury" can then come to a judgment.

There is Konstantin Gavrilovich Treplev, the young writer. He is first introduced to the audience in a dialogue with his uncle, the retired civic councillor. In a later scene the old man says of himself that all his life he had "wanted," unsuccessfully: first, he had wanted to be a writer; then a good speaker; later a married man; and he had wanted to live in the city. (And here the doctor says, "I wanted to become a civil councillor, and I did become one. . . .") The old man is full of sympathy for the revolutionary ideas of the young writer who projects onto the stage the young generation's protest against the corrupt,

played-out theater of yesterday. The kind of theatrical writing that Treplev is doing "portrays life not as
it is and not as it should be, but as we see it in our
dreams."

Seven years later Hugo von Hofmannsthal was to
write a famous essay, *Die Bühne als Traumbild*
("The Theater as Dream Image"). Edward Craig was
to carry out a similar vision of a theater of the future:
he was to design rooms that do not exist and never
will, rooms that our imagination might project. And,
in 1923, the sixty-year-old Stanislavsky was going to
demand that Chekhov's dramas be presented in a
new way. Stanislavsky was then to ask the question,
"Which of us inquired profoundly enough into the
meaning of Treplev's monologue about the nature of
the new art [of the theater]?" What a misunderstanding! Treplev's theater, as Chekhov sees it, was
the theater of the future.

The actress, Treplev's mother, describes it exactly:
Treplev was writing in the manner of those avant-
gardists who were being called "decadents" and had
proudly assumed this label themselves. They heralded
the birth of symbolism. Leonid Andreyev, whose antirealistic abstract *The Life of Man* (produced by
Stanislavsky in 1907) was representative of this movement, was a member of Chekhov's circle of friends.
The younger writers said of Chekhov that he "was
flogging realism to death" (Gorky), and they described what distinguished his theater from the theater of the realists and naturalists as "symbolistic." But
Chekhov said of Andreyev that his work reminded
him of the singing of an artful mechanical nightingale.
Compared with him, Skitalyez, another writer, looked
rather like a sparrow—but Chekhov said he preferred
a real sparrow. The young dramatist in *The Sea Gull*
is accused of not presenting living human beings in

his play; and he exclaims, with derisive defiance, "Living human beings!" No living human beings— that is pure anti-Chekhov criticism! In the "play" that is performed on the stage within the stage the element of satire is clearly recognizable.

In the last act, when Treplev has become a well-known writer, he corrects himself: "Everyday I become more and more convinced that it is not a matter of old and new forms, but that a man must write what is in him, must, without thinking of forms, write freely what is in his soul." This indeed anticipates the ideas of the expressionists—no less than did the earlier "anti-Chekhov": "A writer must be cool. Only coolness makes it possible to maintain objectivity."

And how are we to react to this Treplev on the stage? His concepts are of yesterday and of the day before yesterday. His protest is treated ironically by Chekhov. Are we to join those who laugh at his play so that he becomes angry and with hurt pride stops the performance? Are we to join in with those who declare that everything new is absurd and boring? But Chekhov himself was on the side of protest (against lies), and he defended publicly protesters like Gorky. And he wrote that the public ought to be made aware and afraid: by being confronted with the truth. He himself knew what it was like to feel the loathing of the conservatives: *The Sea Gull*, too, was to be booed off the stage. No, it is not that simple to dismiss Treplev.

Literature, art, and the theater make up the foreground for the dialogue. The views that are expressed cannot be separated from the characters who voice them. They are the means by which each person's individuality is characterized. Treplev expresses anti-Chekhovian views, yet he has been created out of Chekhov's own material. Looking back at his youth, he shares in Treplev's protest. For the rebellion of Treplev is that of the always necessary protest of the young against the generation of yesterday. While Chekhov was writing the play, he observed the protest of a new youth against another yesterday. He so integrated this material into his play that its truth was valid for both generations—that is, the truth behind changing views, the necessary truth of a protesting youth in any epoch.

As we know, it was Chekhov's method to take what he had lived through, experienced, and observed and to use it as material—not simply to reproduce undigested material, but to work with it and make it into a composition. Thus the construction of Treplev is the product both of what Chekhov had lived through himself and what he had observed. Treplev is not only the young writer that Chekhov himself once had been but also a young writer of another generation and another milieu. Treplev's world is the manor house, and the audience that watches his play is country "society." There is a line in which he says that he has been expelled from the university for reasons, "for which the editors refuse to take responsibility." Of another expelled student, one in *The Cherry Orchard*, Chekhov said in a letter that he had been expelled for being a radical—"but how would one say that?" The censor struck out this part of the letter. And so it is possible that Treplev, too, had been expelled for social protest, although it seems that he devotes himself completely to the literary life.

Eventually it becomes clear that literature, art, and the theater are not the true fate of this young man: he only imagines that this is so. In the last act, after he decides to commit suicide, Chekhov gives him a scene in which, for about two wordless minutes, he tears up all his manuscripts. And it is not his fate, as he thinks in the first act, to live in the shadow of his mother, the famous actress, and be degraded, to be a "nothing"—for in the last act he has succeeded in entering the literary world and in making a name for himself. Yet, this achievement now has no meaning for him because of his knowledge that he has failed in love, and he comes to his desperate decision only when he is certain that this failure is final. In these complications Treplev appears as an extremely complicated character, and it is exactly this that makes the character believable and justifies the inevitability of his fate.

Let us look at Treplev's antagonist, the writer Trigorin. He is the man of success, pampered by women, a man seemingly without problems as he acts out a role for himself and others. As a writer, Treplev sees him as a mediocre hack: "He is under forty and already totally satisfied. His literary work? Nice, talented, but if you have read Tolstoy and Zola, you won't find anything in him." But the girl Treplev loves does admire Trigorin's literary work, and Treplev's mother ardently defends his tested talent against the criticism of her son who still merely wants to be a writer and has yet to prove his talent. Surprisingly, Trigorin himself seems to share the view of the young Treplev and his generation, with which of course he is familiar. Is he merely posing when he removes the mask of fame before the young girl and reveals behind it a modest, almost humble face? Chekhov gives him almost the same lines Treplev had earlier: "Quite nice, quite talented, but a Tolstoy he is not." And so, Trigorin says, it was to be all through his life. At his graveside people were to say, "Here lies Trigorin. He was a good writer, but a Turgenev he was not."

Chekhov wants us to think Trigorin intelligent

enough for such insights. They make him likeable. But how do they appear to us later in the light of his behavior toward the girl he has seduced? He is flattered by the admiration of the young so long as it does not obligate him in any way. At the moment the girl begins to be burdensome, he retreats. When he makes his entrance in the last act, it is clear that he has behaved like a swine. His intelligence is coupled with his unscrupulousness, and his insights are as flat and insipid to the taste as are his literary works. Nevertheless at a dramatic point he says the effective lines on which Stanislavsky built his interpretation of the role (which Chekhov vehemently criticized): "I don't have a will of my own, have never had it, am flabby, irresolute, always submissive to others. . . ." When he runs off and leaves the girl with a child, he evidently does have a will of his own.

Stanislavsky asked Chekhov how he saw Trigorin. Chekhov answered, "You must wear shoes with holes in them and checked trousers." Stanislavsky was shocked: "A fashionable writer, the darling of the women—and suddenly checked trousers and torn shoes? I had gotten for the role a most dashing suit and designed beautiful makeup for myself." But one day he suddenly understood: "Just that is the drama, that the women throw themselves on his neck, without noticing that the man is insignificant, without seeing the checked trousers and the torn shoes." Trigorin quite simply is shabby. The successful man in a shabby world.

At the summit of this shabby world stands Arkadina, the celebrated actress, Treplev's mother, Trigorin's mistress and the woman who keeps him. And is she at all capable of loving? Yet Chekhov does justice to her, too. She is not altogether without maternal feelings. They flare up after Treplev has

clumsily put a bullet into his head and she dresses
his wound. He now takes refuge in that long-missed
warmth and says to her, "You have golden hands."
But when her son mocks her cavalier's "refined character," she acts like a fury. It is clear that she feels
mocked herself. She cannot change her style of life.
When Trigorin begs her to give him his freedom, she
plays the great scene of her life. She knows the
weapons that can beat a Trigorin: she flatters his
male vanity; she falls onto her knees before him,
kisses his hand. (Ingmar Bergman, in his Stockholm
production, had the actress look often into the mirror
during this scene.) She says: "My beautiful one, my
wonderful one, my lord. . . ." By no means does she
fight a cool battle. She fights for the triumph of her
beauty, her femininity, her theatrical talent. (And
how tactlessly she has just paraded these means before a young girl that, in this respect, is without
means.) She fights to pit the glamour in her life
against the terrible fear of old age, which is her only
worry. When she again has Trigorin in her power and
feels she can afford to take a risk, Chekhov has her
say, as if nothing had happened: "By the way, if you
want to, you may stay. . . ." How she savors the man's
almost desperate "No, no!"

Chekhov included a repulsive trait in the composition of this character: avarice. In the third act there
is a scene between Arkadina and Treplev, in which
the inner agitation of the two is muffled by the words
that are spoken. This agitation would go unnoticed if
its deadliness did not finally come to light. After
Treplev's suicide attempt, Sorin, Arkadina's sick
brother, tries to appeal to Arkadina's conscience: she
ought to give the boy a little money, a few thousand
rubles. The audience knows that Arkadina has
seventy thousand rubles in the bank. Yet she says,

without pity, "I have no money!" And she repeats this when her brother tells her that he would give the young man the money himself if he had it. She does eventually admit that she has money but asserts that an actress must have her needs gratified. This is too much for her brother to bear. He staggers, breaks down, has an attack.

And Chekhov, with his great knowledge of human nature, ironic to the point of cruelty, continues with this theme, after the sick man is taken away. Now Treplev tells Arkadina that it is bad for his uncle to live in the country, that it would certainly help him if he could move to the city. "I have no money," she replies. "I am an actress, not a banker." When she takes leave, she gives the servants a ruble: "For the three of you." But even while projecting this cruelty Chekhov portrays the actress as a full human being. She suffers great fear of old age. She wants to be alive and to love.

Nina, the Sea Gull, as she calls herself because she is constantly drawn to the lake, is often played as the young girl who is blinded by the glamour of the first famous man she meets and so throws herself into her sad adventure. But Chekhov's character is not that simple. The audience knows that it is a rather shabby glamour to which she falls prey. She has strictly conservative parents (a stepmother to whom her rich father will leave all his money) who have forbidden her to visit the "bohemians" on the neighboring estate. The more irresistible, therefore, is the attraction of their free life. Her head is turned by art, literature, and the stage, long before she experiences love. She allows Treplev to kiss her because he lets her act in his play. Even before meeting Trigorin she is eager to hear all about him. The scene described earlier, in which he disparages the extent of his own talent to effect an appealing modesty, is decisive.

But it is not only his aura that blinds Nina—she herself projects it onto the man. Trigorin is her fate. Chekhov leaves no doubt about it. In the last act, when she, an abandoned woman, goes secretly to the manor house to which Arkadina and Trigorin have returned, Chekhov has her run to the door, through which she hears his laughter, like someone driven. Perhaps she is only trying to convince herself and Treplev that she still loves Trigorin "even more than before." But this is in keeping with her character: to hold on, with the last fragment of her strength, to what she wants. With the same determination which she once brought to giving up her parents' house and wealth in order to go out into the world, for which she then yearned, she now tries to hold onto that wished-for world, though it has treated her wretchedly. Chekhov does not make it clear whether or not she has talent. Even at the moment of farewell, when she deeply wounds Treplev's feelings, she still says that one day she will be "a great actress." Yes, she says, for now that she has learned to bear her cross, she has truly become a great actress. Naturally, for what else is left to her that will let her keep her self-esteem? But Treplev knows the provincial theaters in which she performs, the audiences of small-town men who tend to make importune advances waving their fat wallets. . . .

Each of the characters now is not only what he is intrinsically but also what he has become. There is Masha, for example—whose father is the grumpy estate manager, who can put his foot down because he controls the horses and the cashbox, whose mother unsuccessfully courts the doctor—Masha always wears black and drinks secretly because she is unhappy: her love for Treplev is not reciprocated. But Masha is loved, by a poor teacher, whom she marries. Yet she continues to be drawn irresistibly to the manor house, to the other man. And there is Masha's husband, who speaks of nothing else but his poverty and dotes on his wife with doggish loyalty. He deeply loves her and their children. These characters are not viewed as harshly and critically as were those in *Platonov*. Their humanizing foibles are integrated into their personalities without sentimentality, creating a balance in these wretched characters who do not lack in cruelty.

The plot, too, which is prescribed by the pattern of "the well-made play," is pared down to the indispensable minimum that is needed to arouse interest and tension. In the first act, after the performance of the play within the play is broken off, Chekhov takes one of the indirect steps by which he appeals to the attention of his "jurors": Nina steps before the curtain. She has changed her costume. She is about to meet Trigorin. It is only a brief meeting now, for Nina has only escaped her parents for a brief half hour.

In the second act Nina's parents are away on a trip, and now she can spend the whole day in the bohemians' company. By now Treplev knows what really attracts her to the house, and so he performs a vicious ritual before he appears to meet her again. She had called herself a sea gull in the love scene with him in the first act. Now he shoots a real sea gull. He brings it, to lay it at her feet. As he notices her trembling and radiance as Trigorin approaches, he goes away, to leave the two alone.

After the scene with Trigorin that transports Nina into a state of staggering excitement, the famous man discovers the sea gull. And now Chekhov permits him to make a mistake the ecstatic Nina will not notice, but one that will not escape the attentive "jurors." Trigorin makes a notation in his notebook. "What are you writing down?" asks Nina. "Oh, nothing, just an idea. Material for a little story. There is a girl who lives at the shore of a lake that she loves like a sea gull, and like a sea gull she is happy and free. Then one day a man passes by who notices the girl. He approaches her and destroys her, just so, out of boredom, like this sea gull here was destroyed."

Here, too, Chekhov worked with his own material. Even Trigorin is a piece of himself. One need only go back to the days when Chekhov was still in the process of becoming a serious writer and was writing only for money. Then he, like Trigorin, might have said of himself: "I must write, must write. . . . I have barely finished a story when I have to begin the next one, and then a third and a fourth—I am writing without let-up, as for special delivery. I cannot help myself." We know of the notebooks in which he wrote down "what was usable." They are hardly distinguishable from Trigorin's notebook, into which he, even after the emotional scene with Arkadina, wrote down "a word." "And what are you writing down?" asks Arkadina, much like Nina has asked in the previous act. "This morning I heard a word I would like to use: virgin forest."

In the third act, too, there is talk of the sea gull. It is the act that follows upon Treplev's suicide attempt, in which the actress renews the bandage around Treplev's wounded head. Trigorin walks across the stage. Nina walks across the stage. After the scene with his mother, Treplev runs away, so that he does not have to see Trigorin any more. Now the departure of Arkadina and Trigorin is being prepared. They will return to the city. These two now also have had their great scene. The coach is waiting at the door, and Trigorin returns once more because he has forgotten his cane. Nina is waiting for him, as he knows, and the cane is merely a pretext. She informs him of her decision: "The die is cast, I am going on the stage! I am leaving my parents and going to Moscow. There I shall meet you again. Stay at the Slavic Court and let me know right away when you get there: Moltshalovka, Groholsky House." Then, a long kiss.

Between the third and the fourth act, over a year has passed. What has happened in the interval is quickly told: Treplev has learned what has happened to Nina. He now has everyone's respect, for he has become a successful writer. Arkadina has been called to the estate because her brother is deathly ill, and she brings Trigorin along. Treplev knows that Nina, too, is nearby. When the company retires after supper, he goes out to fetch her, for he knows that she is roaming about outside. He finds out what brings her here. She embraces him after, trembling with excitement, she recites from his play, the play that was performed in the first act. Afterward, when Treplev is alone, he tears up his manuscripts. Then he leaves the house. And the last scene could have been invented only by Chekhov.

The company returns. Candles are lit. They sit down at the game table ("on long fall evenings we play lotto here"). The estate manager takes Trigorin to the cupboard: "There is the thing I told you about. [He takes a stuffed sea gull from the cupboard.] Please, explain its meaning." "I don't remember," says Trigorin. Then, backstage, a shot is fired. "What was that?" Arkadina asks, startled. The doctor answers, "Something probably exploded in my medicine chest. A little glass bottle with ether probably burst."

He hums a melody from an operetta and Arkadina joins in.

Then, while leafing through the pages of a magazine, the doctor grabs Trigorin by the arm, to lead him forward toward the footlights: "This question interests me," he says loudly. And then he adds, in a low voice, "Treplev shot himself."

The Sea Gull, in its premiere on October 17, 1896, in Saint Petersburg, was booed off the stage. On December 17, 1898, in the Moscow Art Theater, it had a triumphal success.

The Three Sisters

A play about hope—and that means a play about time.

Real time differs from stage time because it has neither a beginning nor an end. Even a play that is not divided into acts can only simulate real time, for it has a beginning and an end. Time, arranged within the play, divided into acts and subdivided into scenes, changes its character: its constant passing away. If time is so manipulated, then life, will appear manipulated. A dramatist who wants to show life as it truly is must confront the problem of temporalness and time.

Chekhov did not accept the solution offered to the dramatist by "the well-made play": the three- or five-act model that has its climax in the middle act. For in this pattern life itself is fitted into a model of artificial time. Ibsen was still proceeding in this manner, and most of Shaw's plays, too, still follow this classic scheme. Gorky, however, was strongly influenced by Chekhov, which is evident in his preference for the four-act form. From *Ivanov* on, all of Chekhov's full-length plays are constructed in four acts. It is striking that even in *Ivanov*, which is Chekhov's compromise with "the well-made play," he made no compromise with the realm of time. Chekhov obstinately proceeds according to his experience that stage time of the symmetric model simply cannot be realized on the stage. For the climax, in terms of time, is revoked by the intermission. A true symmetry of stage time would move a play's center into the intermission between the two or four acts. That would mean, however, that the play falls apart into two halves, and that the second half would necessarily appear longer than the first. And so true life time defies standardization.

Although Chekhov's four-act form has to be understood as a conscious countermove against "the well-made play," it is by no means a new pattern that automatically permits the transfer of real time onto the stage. In Chekhov's new form, rather, the problem of time is to be confronted and solved anew and differently in every play. In *Ivanov* and in *The Wood Demon* (and to a certain degree still in *Uncle Vanya*), three acts follow upon each other, while the fourth act is played after an intermission; a greater interval of time thrown between the previous acts elapses between the third and the fourth acts. In *The Sea Gull* there are two breaks in time: between the action of the second and the third acts two weeks have passed, and between the third and the fourth act, two years. Between the first and the second act, also, a few days have passed. Thus it seems that the real time intervals in this four-act play are progressively prolonged. This is exactly in keeping with the truth Chekhov wishes to project: the increasingly more serious results that stem from one definite constellation (here the first act's play within the play).

The structure of *The Cherry Orchard* follows, above all, the seasons. In *The Three Sisters* the seasons also play a part, though here the progression of time serves another kind of truth: the withering of hope reflects the process of aging. The first act takes place at noon on a Sunday in May; the sun stands in its zenith and fills the room with warm light. In the second act it is January the following year, late on a winter evening; candles flicker, and hope is turning toward spring. As the third act begins, four years have passed; it is night, between two and three in the morning, and the ghostly reflection of a fire now and then lights up the stage. In the last act it is again twelve o'clock noon, but now it is fall. We are not told how much time has passed since the previous act and it is unimportant; farewell, death, and buried hope now combine to give us a sense of the kind of time that is to come: the time of aging.

The truth of this time motif derives from the truth of the central idea: three sisters—what could differentiate them more clearly than age? The play begins with the birthday party of Irina, the youngest sister. She has just turned twenty and is the "little one" among the three. It is spring and the end of the year of mourning for their father, the general, who had been the most distinguished person in the society of this garrison town. His house still is the meeting place of his officers, and the salon of the general's daughters is still the town's first and most distinguished.

Olga, the oldest sister, is twenty-eight years old. She wears the Russian civil-service uniform of a teacher. She says of herself that she has aged lately and grown skinny—but her words are not without a note of coquettishness. Among the three, it is Olga who lives most in her memories. Her great longing to return to Moscow—where the sisters spent the years of their childhood before the general's transfer to this garrison town—is by now colored with resignation. She is unmarried, probably also unloved, though, as she says, she could have brought happiness to a man.

With Masha, also, the middle sister, everything is

not as it should be. She is married to a rather ridiculous man whose proposal of marriage she had perhaps accepted too rashly. And this prompts Olga's remark that Masha is the dumbest of the three. But the least intellectual one is also the most feminine. She alone has the experience of a great love, a happiness without future or hope the unfolding of which is presented during the early acts of the play. The man who loves her is also married.

Irina is being courted by two officers, one of them intelligent and plain, the other simple and shy. Despite this rivalry, the two men are friends. But in the last act, a ludicrous provocation triggers a duel between them; the motivation is actually their rivalry for Irina. In this duel the man is killed whose proposal of marriage Irina had finally accepted. From act to act, she becomes older and less spirited.

In this last act the officers all leave town. Among them is Masha's beloved, who has to part from her forever.

There is also a brother, who is a scholar, violinist, and wood carver; yet none of his talents amounts to much. The sisters, nonetheless, have high hopes for him. But he is without energy, and the girl he loves and marries is of a kind that the sisters are disdainful of. But Natasha, the brother's wife, does not live on hope—she knows what she wants and how to get it. One might call her the one positive character in the play if she were not so ruthless, narrow-minded, and petty. As soon as she marries the brother, she becomes the ruler of the household. She takes care that her children have the best rooms in the house. In the third act, she asks Olga and Irina to share a bedroom. In the fourth act, Olga becomes the principal of the hated secondary school where she has been teaching; now she lives at the school. Irina is about to be married. She, too, has become a teacher, and after her fiancé is killed we know that her life will be like that of her older sister, as we have watched it unfold throughout the play.

What it means to be a teacher in a provincial town is illustrated by Masha's ridiculous husband—a man with a limited horizon, without aspirations or intellectual curiosity. He is the only one of the characters who is satisfied with his lot. The brother, who is expected by his sisters, in the first act, to become a university professor, takes a minor municipal post in order to marry. Disappointed by his marriage and henpecked, he becomes a gambler. The unfortunate man gambles away the house. After speaking out once in the third act, he settles back into dullness and self-pity, good for nothing except to push the baby carriage, while his wife carries on an affair, known to all the town, with one of his superiors.

One could say that the officers personify the typical Russians of the *fin-de-siècle*. They wear uniforms that no longer are worn. But nothing would be more erroneous than this interpretation. Chekhov says that this town, this unnamed provincial government seat, is like all other Russian provincial government seats. In the same way the men in the sisters' lives are officers like other Russian officers—that is, "temporal characters." In the beginning there is the hope that one of them will marry one of the girls and take her along when his transfer arrives. But the only thing that is certain is that one day all of them will receive transfer orders. The major event in the first act is the visit the new garrison commander pays the general's daughters. The event of the last act will be the farewell visit: the garrison leaves town. The inaudible yet ever-present "gone by, gone by," that hovers over all the scenes is, one might say, marked upon the officers' foreheads.

And what is this Moscow, on which the sisters put all their hopes? It is a real memory, but heavily embroidered and eventually exposed as an illusion. Eleven years ago they had to leave the scene of their happy childhood, because their father was assigned to a provincial garrison. At the time Olga was seventeen, Masha perhaps thirteen, and Irina a little girl of nine. In the dreary reality of the provincial town, Moscow has become more and more the golden city of their dreams. In the first act they are still quite sure that now that the year of mourning is over, they will soon move back to Moscow. Besides, their brother will surely get a professorship there. What a happy omen they see in the fact that Vershinin, the new colonel, who makes a courtesy call on them, not only comes from Moscow but had even been a visitor to the general's house there (he then was called "the lovesick major"). The dream's golden glow transfigures this man who is now in his early forties and who brings a new note into the usual conversations. A philosopher, he gives the sisters the most beautiful compliments. In the future, he says, in two or three hundred years hence, everything will be different. A happier time will dawn, and "if then, in a desolate, dreary town like this one, there are three human beings like you," that would be proof enough that things are slowly turning for the better. The colonel goes on to say:

> "Of course, you cannot conquer the dull mass around you, and in the course of your lives you will have to forsake, bit by bit, parts of yourselves. Life will smother you. And yet, you shall

not simply fade away, without leaving a trace of light behind you. After you, there will perhaps be six, and then twelve people like yourselves, and so on, until finally human beings of your kind will be in the majority. In two or three hundred years, life on earth will be unimaginably beautiful and grand."

Now, that these trivial ideas are expressed for the first time, the girls hear in them only the note of hope, and the man who says them makes them happy with these words. But in the next act Chekhov has the colonel return repeatedly to this idea. His only conversational topic is this "philosophy," which he trots out at any opportunity—an ironic variation on the play's basic theme. Its contradiction, which others, with opposing arguments, set against it—"life will always stay as it is now, and in two hundred years hence people will sigh as they do now and say, 'How hard life is!' "—is another ironic variation of the same theme. The illusory quality of these conceptions resemble the illusory character of the sisters' Moscow dream, which drives them, as one of them says, "nearly mad." They simply don't listen when the colonel tries to talk them out of their Moscow idea: "People won't even notice that you're there." Moscow is a city like others, life there is just as it is everywhere else; the city of your dream is merely a phantom. By the third act no one listens any longer when the colonel expounds his philosophy. "I think they have all gone to sleep," he observes. And when he starts in on it even while making his farewell, he admits, "I have talked too much—please don't hold it against me!" Subdued, he adds to his chatter about life in two hundred years' time: "If it only would happen sooner!"

To these characters, which reflect the passing of time, Chekhov has added two figures who personify old age. One of these is Chebutykin, the old army doctor, who will soon be pensioned off. He lives in the house of the sisters, whose mother he once idolized. Although he will leave the town with the garrison, he will return to live here in retirement; these are the only people he is close to. This man, too, had faced the abyss. The death of a woman patient under his treatment made him realize his worthlessness. In the third act he gets drunk, trying to forget, but he cannot escape the truth. In the fourth act he is the only one among these unfortunates who has any hope: to return, "and to sit still, traraboomdara." And the other old person becomes perfectly happy— Anfisa, the aged nurse, who had been a target of the sister-in-law Natasha's cruelty and been dismissed from the house. She finds a place in the school, in Olga's apartment, and it is the best place there is for her. "Everything is paid for by the state, and when I wake up in the night, oh dear Lord Jesus and Mother of God, there isn't a happier person than I!"

There is another theme that shows how Chekhov demolishes his characters' ideas, dreams, and desires with his irony. In the first act he has Irina say, "One must work. . . . How I would like to be a worker who gets up at sunrise and hammers the stones into the road, or a shepherd, or a teacher, or a train engineer."

The lieutenant she is engaged to who loves her (who knows that she does not return his love, who fights the duel over her and is killed) is fired by her enthusiasm: "How well I can understand your feelings. . . . Something powerful is in the making, a cleansing storm is about to break upon us. We can feel that it's near, it will soon sweep away all our soci ety's indolence and indifference." And he, who is a baron, continues, "I will work; in twenty-five or thirty years' time simply everyone will work, without exception."

But the man who says these words does not believe in the truth of this idea, yet he wants to realize it for himself, personally. He leaves the army in order to run a brickyard. And he wants to take Irina there, now that she finally consents to become his wife. He says goodbye, "just to go to town for a moment." Shortly thereafter, he is dead.

And Irina? From the second act on, she really does work; as a telegraph operator, as a secretary, and just before the last act begins she passes her teacher's examination. None of these jobs brings her any happiness. Is it the Moscow dream that makes her so unfit for life? This does not mean that Chekhov intends to satirize the idea of work; innumerable times he called indolence and ignorance the most disastrous roots of human wretchedness. Neither is the baron's prophecy meant to be ironic, just because it will be contradicted by his own fate. Chekhov also uses truth itself as material; and truth is not disproved because a man dreams a false dream. But the quintessence of this play that is about the temporal quality of life is not the truth about images and ideas—but the truth about life. And so the final scene of the play, like its first one, shows the sisters together, at the end of all hope. Through Chekhov's irony they have become illuminated to the point of being symbols.

> MASHA: We stay behind, to begin our lives anew. One must live, live.
> IRINA: Some day people will understand why all this is necessary, what the purpose is of all this suffering. . . . But until then we must live. . . .

We must work, we must do nothing but work.
. . . It is fall now, and soon winter will come
and cover everything with snow. And I shall
work, work.

OLGA: Dear sisters, nothing is yet at its end. We
shall live! And it seems to me that it cannot
be too long before we shall know what we are
living for and why we suffer. Oh, if we only
knew, if we only knew!

Masha's husband, the teacher, the contented one,
comes out of the house now, smiling cheerfully. In
the background the brother is pushing the baby carriage past the house. And the old doctor is quietly
humming, "Traraaraboomdara . . . it's all the same."

OLGA: If we only knew, if we only knew. . . .

This play has the character of a chamber-music
composition. In order to counterpoint the dialogue in
the manner of a fugue, the playwright specified that
a stage set consisting of two rooms be the setting for
two acts. A large dining room at the far end of the
stage is separated by pillars yet connected with the
salon that is in the foreground. Often there is action
and dialogue in both rooms simultaneously. In their
coming and going the characters occasionally are not
aware or do not take notice of each other. Somewhere someone sits drinking tea near the samovar,
somewhere else someone is reading a paper, and in
another corner a game of solitaire is in progress.
And so develops the meshing texture of the dialogue
that not only projects what is said but also what the
characters would like to convince themselves of.
Even more, one sees how often each of them is talking past the others.

The external events serve to bring to the surface

the characters' subterranean reactions. Irina's birthday party in the first act fills them all with such happiness that they don't see the grim reality that is beginning to reveal itself.

In the second act a kind of "carnival" takes place. Masqueraders are expected—yet the door is shut to them. Neither is joy permitted to enter. With a candle in her hand the petty bourgeois Natasha, like lady Macbeth—as Chekhov himself has observed —goes through the rooms.

The third act takes place while a great fire is raging in a section of the town. The fire alarm is heard in the distance, and occasionally a red glow hovers on the stage. The setting is the bedroom of the two sisters. Their beds are screened off from the center of the stage. Outside in the hall are neighbors who had to flee from their homes. Yet, despite this grim background, the conversations continue much as they went on in the previous act, which now imbues them with a ghostly quality. News comes that the whole garrison is to be transferred. But nothing matters— just to go to Moscow, not to stay here! For Moscow is all the beauty in the world. . . .

In the fourth act the stage is virtually ripped open. We now see the river in the woods, where the duel will take place, the garden, and the terrace. Passersby are seen in the background where the brother is pushing the baby carriage. The dialogue flits by swiftly. The pauses, as always in Chekhov, heighten the tension. Farewell. Death. The end. "One must live, live."

The Three Sisters had its premiere at the Moscow Art Theater on January 31, 1901, and was received with moderate applause. It is Chekhov's most frequently performed play.

The Cherry Orchard

The time is that in which Chekhov is writing, 1903.

The cherry orchard is part of an estate of a member of the old aristocracy. For years, the lady who owns it has lived abroad. Now her return is awaited. She has used up the money on which she has lived since the death of her husband, who was an attorney, and of her little son—she lost them both in the same year. The estate, on which her brother lives, is overloaded with debts and is soon to be auctioned off. And now a practical man of the world of business, a peasant's son who has achieved some wealth and position, tells the noble masters how they can rescue themselves financially. He suggests that the land of the estate be parceled into lots, and that villas be built on them. Its position by the river and near the railroad station is favorable. If this is done, the rents would yield a good income. The old manor house, of course, whould have to be torn down, and the cherry orchard felled.

But that very idea makes the proposal unbearable. There must be another way out! There is a rich aunt. Perhaps, the daughter will marry into money. But on the day of the auction all these bubbles burst. The estate is sold. After the debts are paid a little money is left over, but it will not last long.

The rich, new owner is the man who proposed the

plan for putting the estate back on its feet: now he himself will realize it. While the old masters take farewell forever of the manor house and the cherry orchard, the first blows of the ax are falling.

Stage time can, to quote Chekhov, not feign real time. Stage time has its own reality; it changes the character of real time, its constant passing away, when it becomes material that is used in a play with a beginning and an end. And so the problem of time has to be dealt with anew in every play. The concept of time will change according to a play's theme. As the stage time in *The Sea Gull* was designed to flow from a particular event in a kind of progression, with increasing intervals between the acts, so the stage time in *The Three Sisters* relates to the transitory quality of life, to aging, to saying goodbye to youth, to the withering of hope. In *The Cherry Orchard* Chekhov attempts his most ambitious endeavor, for the concept of time is the concept of history. Here the theme is the end of an era and the beginning of a new one: the moment of changing epochs. In this moment which is today—that is, Chekhov's present— yesterday and tomorrow collide. The change is irrevocable, whatever it may be called: progress, destruction, fate, or history.

Just as the stage has its own stage time, so it also presents, of course, not real people but stage characters. Just as real life can only be used as material and theme in stage time, so stage characters can only reflect the effect that historical change has upon the people who live through it. Chekhov chooses the human beings from whom he models his characters from the wealth of his life's experiences. He himself is one of his sources, though that is never obvious in Chekhov's writing. He chooses people for their suitability to his theme, and he collects and sets them in a particular place that allows the theme—which is change in *The Cherry Orchard*—to best be presented.

The stage reality does not simply stand for reality. Rather, it has been chosen for its demonstration value, its applicable material, for real people can provide the characters only the texture of their lives. Chekhov's contemporaries were right when they (like Gorky) accused him of "flogging realism to death." But they were wrong when they interpreted his new method of presenting reality on the stage as "symbolistic." The Cherry Orchard was not a symbol to Chekhov. But it is a symbol to the characters in his play who have made it into one.

Twice in the play, in dramatically heightened moments, a mysterious sound is heard: "A distant tone, as if out of the sky, like the sound of a breaking string." Chekhov said that he had heard such a sound as a boy on the shores of the Don, and that it came from a pail falling to the ground in a coal mine. The sound in itself is not mystical; but its eeriness startles people who then make it into a mystery. Therefore Chekhov utilized, for his own ends, the possibility that such a sound can exist and have this effect.

The theme of *The Cherry Orchard* requires that the persons represented in it are characterized to reflect their attitudes toward the changing times. Yet, according to Chekhov himself, these attitudes only have validity when they truly express individual and societal limitations. Each of the characters is what his station of birth destined him to be and also what he himself has become. This truism cannot be ignored when we want to understand Chekhov's aim of presenting a theme on the stage in order to get the audience to perceive the truth. The spectator, of course, is supposed to seek for truth not only in the attitude of each of the characters toward the changing times, but also in the distinctive behavior which each character responds to the same event with. Chekhov's objectivity draws the audience's attention to the fact that an irrevocable process that cannot be stopped, regardless of one's positive or negative attitude toward it (depending on how oneself is being affected by it), has a different impact on different people. And this must be kept in mind if the whole truth is to be perceived. This means that it was Chekhov's intention not to represent the change from a particular old to a particular new time but rather to demonstrate how changing times in general affects people. This is how the Greeks and how Shakespeare understood the meaning of history. Chekhov's particular daring lies in his use of his own time, as material for projecting this theme.

A soviet literary historian called *The Cherry Orchard* Chekhov's "most optimistic play." One could, however, just as well interpret it as his most pessimistic play, as Stanislavsky had done when Chekhov said that he "had ruined his play." One can sentimentalize the play by identifying with the mourning of some of the characters for the decline of their age. Or one can ideologize it through identification with the views of those characters who presage the new times. Both attitudes are wrong. It is clear that Chekhov himself shared neither the mourning of the first nor the hope of the second. Doubtless, in private he had his own definite views. (And it is certain that at the time when *The Cherry Orchard* was written, two years before the revolution of 1905, he considered revolution in Russia irrevocable and desirable.)

But as a dramatist Chekhov was faithful to his intention not of giving a solution to a question but rather of precisely formulating a question so that the audience, "the jurors," could make their own deci-

sions. Whether this judgment was to be like that of
Stanislavsky or like that of the quoted Soviet scholar
was something Chekhov wished to leave open. He
once said that a writer should not write for the future,
for he does not know it, and that the truth can only
be said about what one knows—the present. He insisted that only the case was to be presented on the
stage, not the judgment.

The choice of the play's characters is proof of this
objectivity. For not only is the change of a certain
yesterday to a certain tomorrow brought before our
eyes but also a change of day before yesterday to
yesterday, and from tomorrow to day after tomorrow.
Feers, the aged servant, looms like a fossil of the day
before yesterday in the play's world of Chekhov's
present day. No one but Chekhov could have created
this character as he is—touching, despite his incredi-
ble narrow-mindedness. For Feers the days of feudal-
ism were and are still the golden era. "Before the great
misfortune came upon us, everything was better," he
once says. And what is this "misfortune"? The aboli-
tion of serfdom, in 1861, is what Feers means, who
had been a serf himself until that year. But what
about Feers's counterpart, the manservant who repre-
sents the day after tomorrow? Uprightness here is
mirrored in cynicism, and that perhaps again in uprightness. At the end of the play the aged Feers, the
man of the day before yesterday, stays behind, forgotten by the people of yesterday as if he were a
piece of the house that is about to be torn down.

The tomorrow of *The Cherry Orchard* is not the
revolution but the era of capitalism: Lopahin, the new
owner, is a bourgeois with the nature of a peasant.
Part of the material out of which this figure is forged
comes from Chekhov himself: "I still remember when
I was a boy of fifteen, my father, who is now dead,

he then had a small shop here in the village, hit me so hard in the face with his fist that the blood streamed from my nose." Chekhov wrote: "How can one be against progress if one lived through a time when people were flogged and is now experiencing the present time when the floggings have been stopped?"

Chekhov upbraided Stanislavsky for wanting to present Lopahin as a despicable person: "He is a decent man, in every sense of the word. He strives to behave well and he is intelligent. Don't forget that he is loved by Varya, who is a serious and religious girl." Only the people of yesterday and those who mourn with them for the passing of their time can think of him as brutal. His most individual attribute is shyness. He, the successful man, feels small, even paltry, when he faces a woman. Surely he feels, though he does not admit it to himself, something like love for the grand lady from whom he takes the estate. And there is a note of defiance in his conduct, although the project he will now undertake was originally conceived by him for her benefit: "I have bought the estate on which my father and my grandfather were slaves, and not even good enough to be let into the kitchen."

The characters who belong to the time of tomorrow are a mixed group. There is Varya, who must always have some work to do, who does not trust that she can take her fate into her own hands. She is, in Chekhov's words, a religious crybaby. Then there is the bookkeeper, who always stumbles over his own legs and allows his girl to be snatched away under his very nose.

The characters of the time of the day after tomorrow are similarly varied. Their main speaker is Trofimov, the perennial student. Those who look upon the play as optimistic claim that his lines reflect

Chekhov's views. Surely there is truth in this position. "We must work" in order to reach the goal.
That, in order to do so, the cherry orchard has to be
sacrificed is of no importance to him. Surely it is not
quite justified to accuse Trofimov of idleness. The reason that he has been twice expelled from the university
is undoubtedly political. Yet his ideology seems curious when he maintains that he has no time for
banalities: "We are above love!" For it is understood
that Anya (the daughter of the lady who owns the
estate), who repeats his ideas, is not in love with
them but with Trofimov himself.

Yet Trofimov is the capitalist's true adversary, and
he has his great scene when he refuses to accept
money from him. "I am a free person. And everything
you hold so high and dear, all of you, rich men and
beggars alike, doesn't have the least bit of power
over me. . . . Mankind is marching toward the most
sublime truth, toward the most sublime happiness,
and I am marching among its first columns!" Will
mankind in its sublime happiness "be above love"?
Anya, who wants to work toward this "new, marvel-
ous world," proves the opposite.

There is also the young manservant Yasha, quite a
man, who takes what he fancies and discard what he
no longer wants—he too is a man of the day after
tomorrow.

In the foreground, a soft light falls upon the people
of yesterday, who veil themselves in their illusions.
They gush enthusiastically and dream and float like
ghosts through their lives. What are they to each
other? What do they do for one another? How do
they look when they take off their beautiful masks?

There is Gaev, the aristocratic brother of the lady
who owns the estate, a charming, affable parasite, "a
good-for-nothing" as the old servant calls him, a

fifty-year-old who has never done any serious work until the estate's ruin forces him to take a job at a bank. As he says ironically, he now will become a capitalist.

Foremost among the people of yesterday is Ranevskaya herself, the owner of the cherry orchard, whom everyone, even Trofimov the revolutionary, idolizes. Wherever she appears, Ranevskaya is the central figure. It is as if Chekhov, feature by feature, slowly lets us perceive the truth about her. All our compassion turns to her when we hear that she had left the cherry orchard (and Russia) in utter despair after she lost, one after the other, her husband and her only son. Now she admits that she had been unfaithful to her husband, who had consequently become an alcoholic. She becomes convinced that the child's death was her punishment. But has she learned a lesson from this? Her brother speaks harshly of her, saying that she is depraved, that the life she has led in Paris and on the Riviera cannot be called anything but dissolute, however much she may sentimentalize it. There is no doubt—and Chekhov is discreet enough to communicate this by intimation— that the young manservant, whom she has brought home and who will accompany her when she returns to Paris, where she goes with her last bit of money, is more than just an attendant.

In the last act, Lopahin, the peasantlike bourgeois, says, "We play our parts before each other and life goes on." And so it always will be: one lives and one playacts life. One is happy to see the cherry orchard again and one playacts this happiness. One sits and dreams on an evening in the garden and talks past the others. Each is talking of himself and, at bottom, for himself. And one plays the games at hand: the evening the estate is to be auctioned off, there is a

ball! And so they dance atop their own ruin. Always
they are at the border of the grotesque, yes, even the
absurd. One of the characters has the habit of constantly marking billiard moves. Alongside the young
manservant, who puffs on the biggest cigars, there
goes the one who always stumbles over his own legs.
And one of the women runs through the house carrying a big bunch of keys; she is so busy that she ac-
complishes nothing. And then there is the most
peculiar of all the characters, the loneliest of them
all, one who playacts to herself that she means something to each of the others when she entertains them
with artistic magic tricks. During the ball, before the
news that the estate has been auctioned off arrives,
these scenes take on the character of the ghostly.

Mood and atmosphere never are indicated for their
own sakes. It is not an atmospheric play, but a cool
and cruel one (as Gorky has said of another Chekhov
play). Nevertheless, despite this coolness and this
cruelty, sympathy and laughter are aroused in the
audience. Chekhov became irate when it was reported to him during rehearsals that the play aroused
much weeping: "But where are these characters who
are weeping? It is only Varya, who is by nature a
crybaby."

In the first act, in the gray light of dawn, the windows are opened and we see the blossoming cherry
orchard. When the sun rises, and we hear a shepherd's flute in the distance, nothing could be more
deceptive than this idyllic scene, set up only to be
destroyed. Similarly, in the second act, the characters
"all meditative and thoughtful," enjoy the summer
evening, while the dialogue makes it increasingly
clear that most of them are estranged from each
other, and that even those who have paired off know
and want to know nothing about each other. In the

third act—now fall has come—this double meaning of the scenic conception becomes quite clear: what a cruel invention is this ball at the abyss. In the fourth act the tempo of departure and breakup, blended with sounds backstage, drives the people, who are freezing in the bitter-cold winter (the house is not heated), off the stage. Finally only the aged, forgotten Feers is left behind.

And now is heard for the second time the sound of the snapping string. It recalls the eerie moment in which it was heard before, at the end of the second act, when all those who now are gone were daydreaming and pensive. In addition, in that earlier scene there suddenly popped up a figure who has no particular relevance to the play: a stranger, a tramp, a drunk, who asks for the way to the station, and begs for a small coin "for a hungry Russian." He receives a gold piece and goes off, humming a volga song.

There is nothing sinister or gruesome about this tramp. But at his appearance, the people are startled and frightened, just as they are by the strange sound that "came out of the sky."

Fearfulness and dread: this is the basic atmosphere of a *comédie humaine* set between two epochs in time.

The premiere of *The Cherry Orchard*, the only one Chekhov attended after the failure of *The Sea Gull* in Saint Petersburg, took place on January 17, 1904, six months before his death.

One-act Plays

Chekhov wrote a number of one-act plays. Several of these, such as *Swan Song* (1887–88; also entitled *Kalkhas* after the short story on which it is based) and *A Tragedian in Spite of Himself* (1890), are plays about the theater itself. Most of the one-acters were written at the time when Chekhov was eager to prove to himself and to others that, if he wanted to, he could master the genre of the conventional theater. It is evident that these one-acters are closely related to his short stories. At the time, his short pieces in dialogue form, which were published in the newspapers, were also very popular. Among these was the short monologue *On the Harmfulness of Tobacco*, which he wrote six versions of, the first in 1886 and the last in 1902.

Tatyana Repina, a strange play, a work done to order as a continuation of a historical play by his friend Suvorin, was written in 1889. Besides the brief *On the Highway* (1885), *The Night before the Trial* (1890), and *The Anniversary* (also translated as *The Jubilee*), there are the masterpieces *The Bear* (1888), *The Proposal* (1888–89), and *The Wedding* (1890). These one-acters were very successful in Chekhov's lifetime and are still being performed today.

Chekhov called most of his one-acters "vaudevilles," the French word for the genre of the French theater that at the time was so popular in Russia. These short works can well be described as sketches or farces. Chekhov wrote his one-acters for his own enjoyment, and he once said that he could write these pieces effortlessly, by the dozen. "What can you do when your hand itches to write some tra-la-la for the stage!" Yet there are also such quotes as This: "Thanks to circumstances, I've been busy writing a stupid vaudeville, and thanks to the circumstance that it's stupid, it's a success." He advised a fellow writer in 1895 to get himself a parrot who then could call out to him every day, "Write vaudevilles, write vaudevilles!"

The Bear is a variation on the theme of *The Widow of Ephesus*. In it a young widow decides to mourn until death for her husband who died half a year before. And this although he had cheated on her or, rather, because of it—for she wants to make him ashamed posthumously. She is cured by an intruding creditor, who comes to collect money the dead man owed him and whom she is determined to get rid of without payment. The cure takes place involuntarily. After pursuing his aim for a good while and behaving like an uncouth bear, the intruder is finally overawed, overpowered by the energy of his female opponent. And so he falls into an opposite stance: "What a woman! I've never seen anything like her!" He makes her a proposal of marriage; indignant, she retreats. He is about to depart: "You're not willing? All right— then it won't be!" Now, calling out, "I hate you!" she throws her arms around his neck. The servants, who had been called to throw the bear out of the house, stand by bewildered, looking on at the kissing pair.

In *The Proposal*, the comic turns and crises develop out of the idiosyncrasies of the characters. The girl

is quarrelsome, the young man a capricious, hypochondriac crank. When they are left alone, there are
so many silly quarrels that the young man doesn't
have a chance to state his request. It is to make his
request that prompted him to present himself in his
dress suit.

When he reaches a stage of high fury and is about
to leave, the girl finally hears from her father what
had prompted the visit. "A proposal? Hold him here!
Bring him back!" He returns, and now the quarreling,
again about a trifle, becomes ever sharper. At this
point the young hypochondriac falls into a faint. The
father offers the half-dead suitor a glass of water and
screams, when the young man regains consciousness,
"You had better marry quickly—or the devil take
you!" The two lovers sigh and sink into each other's
arms. But as the father calls for champagne, they are
at it again. As the curtain drops, the laughing audience thinks, what a marriage that will be!

The Wedding is a satire about the petty bourgeoisie's rage for status. The scene is the milieu of
Chekhov's hometown, Taganrog. Shortly before writing this one-acter, he had traveled to the south, to
visit the places in which he had spent his childhood.
He knew the characters he had assembled for the
wedding feast—low-ranking civil-servants, merchants,
sailors. It is not by accident that the bridegroom is a
Greek named Aplombov, a member of the more affluent, upper strata of this society. But the strokes with
which Chekhov draws this milieu are only decora-
tions on the major theme, which is the object of the
satire. The bridegroom has been promised that among
the wedding guests will be a general. Desperately,
the bride's family searches for such an illustrious man
and finally comes up with a sea captain. At the

wedding feast, he is treated with enormous respect, and eventually he dominates the conversation. He so bores the party with his sea stories that everybody begins to grumble. Incensed and offended, he leaves the hall. Now, the party can really begin.

These one-acters are often produced as Russian genre plays. But, as always with Chekhov, the milieu is only the material from which he takes off. The comic elements spring from the characters' human foibles and weaknesses, which by no means are merely Russian characteristics. The sparkling freshness and sauciness of these farces only come out when the humor and laughter breaks through the foreground of the milieu. And only then can the cool irony of these compositions come into its own.

STAGE PRODUCTIONS
IN EUROPE

Chekhov was and is still the great dramatist of the Moscow Art Theater. To this day its emblem is the sea gull. On its foreign tours, the Moscow
Art Theater still presents Chekhov productions that
have been in its repertoire, almost unchanged, for
decades. The merits and misinterpretations in these
productions I have discussed earlier. It was Chekhov's view that Stanislavsky was "ruining" his plays.
But Stanislavsky's productions of Chekhov did not
simply remain as they were being played during
Chekhov's lifetime or shortly after his death. Meyerhold reported that Stanislavsky's mania for stage detail reached absurd proportion in his second production of *The Sea Gull*, and that in his second production of *The Cherry Orchard*, in the departure scene
of the third act, he had a real troika and horses
brought onto the stage.

Yet Stanislavsky's memoirs make it clear that he
became more and more concerned with bringing out
"the line of the inner dialogue" (rhythm and melody), and with cutting down on his old tendency to

scenic naturalism. In the last of the many chapters he devotes to Chekhov, Stanislavsky himself demands a revision of the traditional style of producing Chekhov—"a new Chekhov." What degree of perfection the Moscow Art Theater ensemble achieved in their interpretation of Chekhov's "art of the quiet truth" may be gathered from a review written by the German critic Alfred Kerr in 1922—only a few years before the publication of Stanislavsky's memoirs.

Here is Kerr's reaction to a guest performance of the Moscow Art Theater then on tour in Berlin:

> A true performance. . . . Simply wonderful. . . . How the people come and go (they don't seem to be characters making stage entrances) . . . how they stroll through the rooms! One comes from here, another from there, and so there they are. . . . The whole thing is superb, superb, superb. . . . It's a jewel, and truly human. A reflection of life on earth. . . . It is not the individual actor who matters but the marvelous meshing together, one into another. . . .

For the Russian revolutionaries who, around 1910, proclaimed their anti-illusionism, the Chekhov theater —just because it was Stanislavsky's theater—became the prototype of the dated style they opposed. On the tenth anniversary of Chekhov's death (in 1914), Mayakovsky had saluted the author as a master of language—of "laconism, concentration, and precision." In 1921, for the prologue to the second version of his futuristic play *Mysterium Buffo*, he wrote:

> In other theaters too they have representation, but for them the scene is merely a keyhole. One sits still and watches how in this play a highly

developed alien life is dismembered. One sits still and watches and hears Uncle Vanya snuffle and converse with Aunt Marya. But we are not interested in uncles and aunts, secretly we ourselves have our dear relatives at home. Surely we show plays taken from common and real life only to let the theater heighten it into the realm of the uncommon.

After the Revolution it was the official judgment that Chekhov was "too objective," and therefore dated (to quote Lunacharsky, commissar for art and education in 1922). In the 1934 edition of the Soviet encyclopedia this negative judgment was formulated in such terms as "static," "lacking in action," "without ideas," and "a translation of the art of impressionist painting, of the accidental, into drama." Even Meyerhold now disavowed the playwright he had once loved so dearly.

It was not until the period in which the theater put itself at the service of promulgating the objectives of the 1917 revolution ended that a change came about. And this indeed was a strange change. Now Chekhov was proclaimed the precursor and prophet of the Revolution. His plays were interpreted as optimistic; he was discovered (especially by Yermilov) as the great writer who had swept away the cobwebs of the old. After Stalin's death, this kind of Chekhov fashion also came to an end.

Characteristic of the present Soviet attitude toward Chekhov is the 1961 essay by Ilya Ehrenburg, "On Re-reading Chekhov," that I have previously referred to. This is a splendid analysis and an unreserved acknowledgement of Chekhov.

Outside Russia, usually following the immensely successful tours of the Moscow Art Theater, Chekhov's work has found a warm reception. Especially in northern Europe, in Holland, and in the English-speaking countries, there has developed a lively Chekhov tradition, modeled after Stanislavsky. This Chekhov tradition has greatly influenced both dramatic writing and the performing arts. Clearly, the concept of "the understatement" is rooted in Chekhov's "art of the quiet truth," as it was developed by the Moscow Art Theater. G. B. Shaw called himself a Chekhov disciple. The relationship of such contemporary English dramatists as Harold Pinter, John Arden, John Mortimer, and Arnold Wesker to Chekhov's indirect method has been pointed out by John R. Taylor in his book *Angry Theater: New British Drama*. To this day the major Chekhov roles are among the favorites of such distinguished actors as Lawrence Olivier. Such great Swedish and Finnish directors as Olof Molander and Eino Kalina, whose Chekhov productions have been highly praised, have called themselves disciples of Stanislavsky.

In France, as late as 1939, however, Pitoëff—who had gone there from Russia via Switzerland—was to find out that Chekhov was a little-known author. The Pitoëffs' contribution was decisive in radically changing this situation. In 1961 the French magazine *Arts* spoke of Chekhov as the most often produced playwright in France! Chekhov clearly has influenced Giraudoux and Anouilh. François Mauriac compared him with Mozart. Jean-Louis Barrault said that in Chekhov "every moment is full. And this fullness does not lie in the dialogue but in the silence, in the sense of life." It was Jean Vilar who first brought *Platonov* onto the stage, and he himself played the title role. It would be interesting to seek out Chekhov's trail in the works of Samuel Beckett.

The German theater, too, around 1918, had a short

Chekhov period. Surprisingly, the only Chekhov play ever directed by Max Reinhardt was *The Bear*, in 1905. The theaters he managed, however, sponsored Chekhov productions that left deep impressions, such as the impression the 1917 production of *The Sea Gull* (directed by Eugen Robert) made on the critic Siegfried Jacobson. Jacobson wrote: "One follows with compassionate interest, a response that makes one more attentive than the suspense that is elicited by the usual obvious plot, how bonds of love and suffering are tightened and undone between all these people. Chords are sounded that are familiar to us all."

In 1919, at the Volksbühne, Jacobson saw *The Cherry Orchard* (directed by Kayssler). He wrote:

> This artlessness will survive the artfulness (of an Ibsen) and literary fashions. It's an example of timeless poetry. . . . *The Cherry Orchard* is inhabited by a dozen people who itch and squirm, quarrel and love, rise and fall, rule and serve, are full of desire and full of resignation— are born and die. It is a moving reflection of our own existence. . . . They are all little people with everyday destinies. Their conversations do not strive to be intellectually representative. How great must have been Chekhov's genius, his sensitivity, his knowledge of the human soul, his ability to illuminate it, his gift to feel his brother's suffering and capture it.

But Chekhov did not take root in the German-speaking theater. And this, although he was loved deeply by Jürgen Fehling, who directed the premiere of *The Three Sisters* in 1926, and Heinz Hilpert, whose last production, in 1967 in Munich, was that of a Chekhov play. This, in part, can be attributed to the difficulty of translating Chekhov into German. But the main reason is that "the art of the quiet truth," as Stanislavsky was presenting it in his later years (German productions, directed by Stanislavsky's student Peter Scharoff, were also being offered) arrived on the German stage at the time when Brecht's theater demanded that the truth be made "spectacular" in order to prevail. And Thomas Mann's "Anton Chekhov: An Essay," published in 1954, did not succeed in bringing Chekhov any closer to the German audience.

It is possible that there now will be a change. For throughout the world, theater people are beginning to realize the need for a long overdue revision of the Chekhov theater.

I have already mentioned five productions as examples of such new interpretations. High standards for a new Chekhov theater have been set by Giorgio Strehler's 1959 Milan production of *Platonov* and by Ingmar Bergman's 1961 Stockholm production of *The Sea Gull*.

In 1967, the Czech director Otomar Krejča created a sensation with his production of *The Three Sisters* at Prague's Theater before the Gate.

Krejča says that Chekhov is "cool like a surgeon." Because of the relentless objectivity and "extreme justice" with which Chekhov treats his characters' attitudes, thoughts, and emotions (also their hardly conscious and unconscious ones), Krejča believes he has the right to move his actors about as if they were driven in harness. It is he, the director, who causes them to move about, clearly against their own will—and this subjugation mirrors how the play's events affect the characters. And the effect of this subjugation is that the actors are put into a state of high tension. Here Chekhov's silence is hardly part of the stage directions. It is rather a dismantling of the spoken words through that which happens behind, between, and beyond them. Krejča does use Stanislavsky's method of direction, but his objective is not to create a constant and noisy atmosphere or to express "inner" dialogue through silent acting. Here the sounds thicken, jelling into surrealist music. The gestures, the walking, swing in its rhythm, and the constant play of movement and expression that underlies the dialogue becomes high-tension choreography. The Prague *Three Sisters* so far is the richest example of a revision of the Chekhov theater.

In his Stuttgart production of *The Three Sisters* in 1965, Rudolf Noelte interpreted, with admirable consistency, "the quiet truth" quite differently from Stanislavsky. Noelte saw the play not in terms of scenic detail but as a distillation. Some critics said, and quite rightly so, that he had projected a Beckett world. Peter Zadek, again quite differently, and also in Stuttgart, in his 1968 production of *The Cherry Orchard*, uncovered another Chekhov truth that Gorky already had spoken of: coolness and cruelty. (One could have done without his rearrangement of the second act, which tampered with the play's characters and its structure.)

Recently, there has been a revealing controversy about the interpretation of Chekhov in Moscow. A production of *The Three Sisters*, directed by Anatoli Efros, was closed down because its unconventional style was clearly opposed to the Stanislavsky tradition and so to socialist realism. W. Bronska-Pampuch reported on this production (in the *Stuttgarter Zeitung*, 1968, No. 50):

Chekhov has been newly discovered. He has, of course, been presented on the Russian stage for decades, but it seems that only now has he been rightly understood. Anatoli Efros, a young director, has produced *The Three Sisters* without the old obligatory sets projecting heavy mood and atmosphere. Gone now is the avenue of birch trees, gone the naturalistic room decor. On the empty stage stands merely a single, stylized tree with copper leaves, which also serves as a coat rack. From the very beginning, Chekhov's characters are now isolated and lonely, and their relationship to the world around them is full of frustration. The ending of the play that in past productions, like many lines of the dialogue, sounded melodramatic, now is farcelike. "Chekhov always wanted to be understood as a writer of farces and comedies," said the Moscow theater critic Maya Turovskaya. "But people didn't take serious notice of such remarks and declared that Chekhov had merely been joking. For this attitude did not fit into the tradition of our Russian theater." Now, finally, there is an effort to do justice to Chekhov, the great renewer. And now the development of the Chekhov tradition, that stopped in the year 1900, begins anew.

STAGE PRODUCTIONS
IN AMERICA

Although there had been isolated productions of Chekhov in America during the first two decades of the twentieth century, widespread interest in Chekhov began with the first visit of the Moscow Art Theater to New York in 1923. Stark Young, distinguished critic and translator of Chekhov, felt as if he were seeing Chekhov for the first time: "I saw Chekhov's art come true, all the strange, incessant flux of it, its quivering and exposed humanity, its pathetic confusion of tragic, comic, inane, and grotesque" (*Immortal Shadows*).

This visit was an introduction for Americans to complex ensemble playing and to Stanislavsky himself, who was to have such an enormous influence on American acting and directing, although Stanislavsky has been almost consistently misinterpreted here. (See Christine Edward's *The Stanislavsky Heritage* for an extensive treatment of the influence of Stanis-

This chapter was specially written by Leonard S. Klein for this American edition.

lavsky in America.) An early emulator of the Moscow Art Theater was Eva Le Gallienne, that indefatigable trooper, who sincerely—but somewhat academically—adopted the ideals of naturalism and ensemble acting in her numerous national touring groups, which performed on and off for the next four decades. Le Gallienne's repertory almost always included a Chekhov play.

For the next twenty years, however, there was little discernible influence of the Moscow Art Theater on Broadway Chekhov productions. Instead of "method" acting or ensemble playing, New Yorkers were given stars, stars, stars. The 1938 production of *The Sea Gull* was conceived as a vehicle for Alfred Lunt and Lynn Fontanne. Stark Young was full of admiration for this production, but Mary McCarthy found lacking any sense of ensemble. She thought the acting of the juvenile roles uniformly poor (including that of Uta Hagen as Nina). McCarthy did admire the older people and singled out for praise "the slick overacting of Lynn Fontanne's Arkhadina" (*Theatre Chronicles 1937–1962*).

Mary McCarthy found the 1943 all-star revival of *The Three Sisters* (Judith Anderson as Olga, Katherine Cornell as Masha, Gertrude Musgrove as Irina, and Ruth Gordon as Natasha, the domineering sister-in-law) more seriously offensive: "[The] production . . . erupts heavily, like a slow volcano, over the topography of the play, so that the playgoer who would like to know what Chekhov was doing here must perform a considerable work of archaeology." Echoing Chekhov's complaints about Stanislavsky, McCarthy observed that "American actors cannot understand why Chekhov called many of his plays comedies." Predictably, the newspaper critics blamed the failure of the production on the play, not on the

sacred cows on stage. A typical judgment was that of
Lewis Nichols in the *New York Times*—"a dull, re-
mote play."

As if in answer to a Broadway prayer, New York
audiences received a gift of instant relevance in 1950,
in the form of *The Wisteria Trees*, described in its
program as "a new American play written and directed by Joshua Logan [a self-styled Stanislavsky
disciple] . . . based on Anton Chekhov's *The Cherry
Orchard*." John Mason Brown, generally an admirer
of Logan, was not impressed by the results: "For
those who have read or seen it and who cherish the
faintest recollections of *The Cherry Orchard*, *The
Wisteria Trees* is bound to suffer from a cruel disad-
vantage" (*Dramatis Personae*). *The Wisteria Trees*,
too, was centered on a star—Helen Hayes—who was
warmly applauded in this simplified version of
Ranevskaya (here called Lucy Andree Ransdell).
The main thing this adaptation showed was that the
similarities between Russia and the American South
(Logan had transplanted the scene of the action to
Louisiana) in the late nineteenth century were only
superficial.

An attempt, at least initially, to break away from
the notion of Chekhov as a star vehicle was David
Ross's cycle of Chekhov plays at the Fourth Street
Theater in the days of off-Broadway's youth—
1955–56. The series began with a star-less production
of *The Three Sisters*, which the major drama critic
Eric Bentley found uneven, mainly in its acting; but
he also observed that the play's "greatness and loveli-
ness come through instead of being obstructed and
whittled away as I remember them to have been in
the grandiose Broadway production of a dozen years
ago. . . . It is made clear that the sisters are small-
town girls, not Park Avenue hostesses in disguise"

(*What Is Theatre?*). The series at the Fourth Street Theater continued with *The Cherry Orchard*, *Uncle Vanya*, and *The Sea Gull*. But each successive production revolved more and more around a star and less around the play.

Two further star-studded productions of Chekhov were presented in New York, during the 1960s. The Actors Studio Theater production of 1964 featured Kim Stanley as Masha and Geraldine Page as Olga. Robert Brustein, then drama critic of the *New Republic*, severely condemned this Lee Strasberg production: "This production will confirm the Philistines in their conviction that Chekhov is a deadly bore. . . . Though the play is only sixty pages of printed text, it takes the Actors Studio Theater three hours and ten minutes to speak it" (*Seasons of Discontent: Dramatic Opinions 1959–1965*). Brustein also noted that jarring conflict of acting styles. No more successful than this production of *The Three Sisters* was John Gielgud's production of the rarely performed *Ivanov* (1966), starring himself and Vivien Leigh (her last New York stage appearance). Stanley Kauffmann, reviewing the production in the *New York Times*, felt that it only emphasized the play's defects: "At its best [the production is] made of smooth surfaces; and its worst is worse than it has any right to be."

America in the 1960s did, however, witness a movement away from the star system and toward ensemble playing, mainly manifested in the growth of regional repertory theaters. Because of the large number of good roles in any of his plays, Chekhov's dramas have been popular with these new companies. Tyrone Guthrie had success in Minneapolis with his 1963 production of *The Three Sisters*. The American Conservatory Theater, based in San Francisco, toured the country with an understated, sensitive production of *Uncle Vanya* in 1966 and a shrill, hectic production of *The Three Sisters* in 1969. New York's APA presented an updated version of *The Sea Gull* in 1962, which looked to Robert Brustein "as though someone had dropped the play in a time-place machine and whirled it in several directions at once." In 1968 Eva Le Gallienne directed a production for APA of *The Cherry Orchard*, which Clive Barnes, drama critic of the *New York Times*, called "respectable, for the most part, but not vibrant."

These American attempts at ensemble playing of Chekhov were put into perspective by a visit, after an absence of over forty years, of the Moscow Art Theater in 1965. Their American repertory included *The Three Sisters* and *The Cherry Orchard*. Although some critics felt that the company now looked old-fashioned, everyone felt that here for once was Chekhov done by an *ensemble*. Actors listened to each other; American actors, including the would-be Stanislavsky disciples, rarely seem to do this.

BIBLIOGRAPHY

Works by Chekhov

Polnoe sobranie sochinenii i pisem A. P. Chekhova.
Russian edition, 20 vols. Edited by S. D. Baluk-
hatyi, V. P. Potemkin, and N. S. Tikhonov. Moscow, 1944–51.

Works about Chekhov

Bruford, W. H. *Chekhov and His Russia.* London,
1947.
Eekman, Tom, ed. *Anton Čechov—Some Essays.*
Leiden, 1960.
Ehrenburg, Ilya. "On Re-reading Chekhov." In *Che-
khov, Stendhal, and Other Essays.* New York, 1963.
Hingley, Ronald. *Chekhov—A Biographical and Crit-
ical Study.* London, 1950.
———. *Russian Writers and Society 1825–1904.* Lon-
don and New York, 1967.
Laffitte, Sophie. *Tchékhov 1860–1904.* Paris, 1963.

————. *Tchékhov par lui-même, images et textes.* Paris, 1955.

Magershack, David. *Chekhov—A Life.* London, 1952.

————. *Chekhov the Dramatist.* New York, 1960.

Mann, Thomas. "Anton Chekhov: An Essay." In *Great Essays by Nobel Prize Winners*, edited by L. Hamalian and E. Volpe. New York, 1963.

O'Connor, Frank. *The Lonely Voice.* Cleveland, 1963.

Simmons, Ernest J. *Chekhov: A Biography.* Boston, 1962.

Struve, Gleb. "On Chekhov's Craftsmanship: The Anatomy of a Story." *Slavic Review* 20 (1961), No. 3.

Triolet, Elsa. *L'Histoire d'Anton Tchékhov.* Paris, 1954.

Winner, Thomas. "Chekhov's *Seagull* and Shakespeare's *Hamlet*: A Study of a Dramatic Device." *American Slavic and East European Review*, January 1956.

————. "Chekhov's 'Ward No. 6' and Tolstoyan Ethics." *Slavic and East European Journal* 17, No. 3.

————. "Myth as a Literary Device in the Works of Chekhov." In *Myth and Symbol*, edited by Bernice Slote. Lincoln, Nebraska, 1963.

————. "Theme and Structure in Chekhov's 'Betrothed.'" *Indiana Slavic Studies* 3 (1963).

WORKS ON AMERICAN THEATER

Bentley, Eric. *What Is Theatre?* New York: Atheneum Publishers, 1968.

Brown, John Mason. *Dramatis Personae: A Retrospective Show.* New York: Viking Press, 1965.

Brustein, Robert. *Seasons of Discontent: Dramatic*

Opinions 1959–1965. New York: Simon & Schuster, 1965.

Edward, Christine. *The Stanislavsky Heritage.* New York: New York University Press, 1965.

McCarthy, Mary. *Theater Chronicles 1937–1962* New York: Farrar, Straus & Company, 1963.

Young, Stark. *Immortal Shadows.* New York: Hill and Wang, 1958.

INDEX